VOLUME I: ISSUE 1

THE GLOBAL CITIZEN

A WORLDWIDE FORUM FOR INTERNATIONAL AFFAIRS

THE GLOBAL CITIZEN: Volume I: Issue 1

THE GLOBAL CITIZEN is published twice a year by Faenum Publishing (Oxford, Ohio, United States). Its Executive Staff is comprised of students and faculty at Miami University located in Oxford, Ohio, United States of America. THE GLOBAL CITIZEN is not an official publication of Miami University and does not seek to represent the viewpoints of its administration.

This Issue is the official Inaugural Release of THE GLOBAL CITIZEN's English Bureau. THE GLOBAL CITIZEN's French Bureau is called THE GLOBAL CITIZEN: DAKAR and is a direct affiliate of THE GLOBAL CITIZEN's English Bureau.

Back cover artwork and artwork accompanying *Debt & Power* and *Refugees on the World Stage* credited to Kim Parent of Miami University. Artwork accompanying *The Political Ripple Effect of 9/11*, *The Obama Doctrine* and *The Rise of Right Wing Nationalism in Hungary* credited to Winston Reid of Miami University.

Information regarding the map on the front cover:
    Vrients, Jan Baptista. *Orbis terrae compendiosa description ex peritissimorum totius orbis gaeographorum operibus desumta.* General Collection, Beinecke Rare Book & Manuscript Library, Yale University in New Haven, Connecticut, United States of America.

Special thanks to Morgan Murray of Miami University, Head Designer on this issue.

Published November 2013 in the United States by Faenum Publishing, Ltd. (Oxford, Ohio)

ISBN-13: 978-1940997032
ISBN-10: 1940997038

TABLE OF CONTENTS

Acknowledgments

No feat is ever accomplished by the efforts of only one person. Success is the product of the efforts of many and the help of many others. And that has certainly been the case here.

There were a lot of obstacles that could have prevented this inaugural issue from being a success. It was only because of the help, guidance and time that others volunteered that have been why this Publication was even possible. For these reasons, the entire staff of The Global Citizen is indebted to all those whose contributions have allowed for The Global Citizen to exist.

In particular, we would like to thank Miami University's Associated Student Government for generously investing in our nascent enterprise in good faith that our Publication would be a success and a hallmark of the University in years to come. We are deeply indebted to ASG for believing in us when all we had to show for our dream was a constitution of who we are and an itemized proposed budget.

We also acknowledge the fact that ASG's funds are not supplied solely by student fees. Donor support is also a part of the funding. We therefore thank Miami alumni and others who donate to the University. Your support has enabled The Global Citizen's staff to grow its international presence and steadily realize its objectives so that the service the Journal provides can be shared with more and more students across the world.

We also extend thanks to Dr. Patrick J. Haney in appreciation for the time and insight he gave which contributed to the development of our Publication since its outset. On top of being interim chair of Miami University's Political Science Department and teaching several courses, Dr. Haney has repeatedly made sacrifices to advise us in the process working toward the production of our first issue in a wise manner.

Next, we would like to thank Senior Lecturer Patti Newberry of Miami University's Journalism Department for advising us on how to establish a solid foundation for The Global Citizen's future. We greatly appreciate her enthusiasm and interest in our Journal's mission and the service we intend to provide the world.

Last, but certainly not least, we would like to thank Miami University for providing us, students, with an intellectually stimulating environment in which we are encouraged to strive for academic excellence. We especially thank the University for encouraging students to innovate and providing the means for students to explore new frontiers in academia and elsewhere. The Global Citizen is a testament to the fact that Miami's administration has truly demonstrated a commitment to helping students grow their competencies outside the classroom. We are encouraged to develop our entrepreneurial drives through the creation of clubs and organizations. The administrative and financial support is there. One just has to dream big enough.

Without the support of the University and faculty members who have been advising us, none of this would be possible. Thank you, again, to all those who contributed to the production of The Global Citizen's first issue. We are tremendously grateful for your continued support.

About The Global Citizen

Millions of young scholars around the world lack a venue through which they can share their analysis on pressing world issues with the rest of the globe. This lack of a strong academic infrastructure is oftentimes due to underdeveloped academic resources and a general culture that promotes work done by Master's and PhD students but seldom those produced at the undergraduate level. In some countries, this lack of access is exacerbated by government control of information — and disinformation — that is disseminated in and out of the country. The young authors in these scenarios come from vastly different worlds and cultural contexts, and approach their education with unique perspectives and ideological convictions. When those experiences are aggregated, those millions of students represent an extraordinary collection of ideas and insights about the way this world works. The Global Citizen exists to create the world's first singular international forum through which the future leaders of the globe can share original, critical analyses of world events and discuss the direction in which the world is headed.

The Global Citizen is an international academic journal edited and managed by a growing network of young scholars around the world who believe in the power they as a generation have to change minds with their insightful works. The Global Citizen provides young scholars from New York to Tokyo, Caracas to London, Sydney to Dakar, and everywhere else in between, with a platform through which they can share their ideas. Twice a year, the Journal publishes the work of the world's best and brightest students in an effort to share their research and analyses to others across the globe interested in international affairs. The Global Citizen publishes works on culture, religion, business and economics, foreign policy, state development and social justice.

The Global Citizen was founded by Winston Reid in the fall of 2012. Its international headquarters and English Bureau are based at Miami University in Oxford, Ohio, United States of America. The French Bureau (called The Global Citizen: Dakar) is run by a staff of African students studying at L'Institut Supérieur de Droit de Dakar and L'Université Cheikh Anta Diop. Both institutions are located in Dakar, Senegal.

Photograph by Marit Lovaas

Dear Reader,

You are holding exemplary work on contemporary international affairs issues from some of the worlds brightest young minds. This Journal seeks to provide the world with a venue by which its young scholarly community can publish such works. I was inspired to found this publication because of my own experience as an undergraduate student interested in international affairs and my realization that a journal of this type has been needed.

Two years ago, I produced a thesis entitled "Redefining Legitimacy and Its Application Into the International System" under the advisement of Levar Smith, a graduate student studying political science at Miami University. I believed my argument to be a compelling one in that it offered a novel approach to understanding how states define 'legitimate governments' in the 21st century and how they ought to approach foreign policy situations where it is not clear which group in a particular country is the legitimate governing body.

I presented my work at two conferences. But after applying to a slew of journals in an attempt to have my work published in an accredited academic publication, I received several rejection letters saying that their respective journals either (a) only publish the work of graduate students; or (b)only showcase the work of their host university's own students. In fact, one journal initially accepted my thesis for further review but, upon learning that the author was an undergraduate, later rejected it. I grew frustrated that there were not many options for me to share my work with the academic community. Even for the undergraduate journals out there, many of them either have a regional focus (for most of these, that means their authors attend only U.S. institutions for the most part) or are run by a particular university. There has not yet existed one single premier publication that does not belong to a single university or country, run by young scholars and young scholars only, disseminates its print publication to every university on the planet with an international affairs program and is privately funded. Well, until now, that is.

I submit that undergraduate students (and scholars in general in their early 20s), who have not yet been heavily exposed to the theories, paradigms and orthodox protocols that make up the educational basis for subsequent levels of higher education, can provide noteworthy analyses on today's most contentious political and economic problems as well as unique solutions to them. Young scholars are in a unique position to use the knowledge they have gained to develop novel viewpoints that may not have been considered before by older academics and experts. This is part of the reason why I not only firmly believe in the quality of work young scholars can produce, but I also believe it to be a critical, valuable contribution to scholars of all ages and from all levels of academia. To that point, I also have developed great faith in the editorial capabilities of undergraduate students. This is due to my experience working with The Global Citizen's English and French Bureau staffs. The English Bureau is comprised entirely of students studying at Miami University, while the French Bureau is made up of students across Francophone Africa studying in Dakar, Senegal.

There is a place for all types of work in the academic arena. Everyone has something to offer. Students in law school, for example, have the knowledge base to produce work that critically examines legal affairs. That is not to say, though, that work from other students is not capable of offering anything substantial to intellectual discourse.

The Global Citizen is on track to being the premier publication in the world to be run by young scholars, be independently funded and publish exemplary works by young academics the world around, especially those who otherwise have no venue through which they can share their insight with the world.

It is my hope that, as you read this journal, you may get a better idea of the caliber of work young scholars are capable of producing, and how their novel approaches can be beneficial to academics as well as all global citizens interested in international affairs everywhere. By reading our publication, may you take away something new that you had not considered before.

Sincerely yours,

Winston Reid
Founder & President of The Global Citizen

It is time for a new generation of leadership,
to cope with new problems and new opportunities.
For there is a new world to be won.

John Fitzgerald Kennedy

VOLUME I: ISSUE 1

THE GLOBAL CITIZEN

A WORLDWIDE FORUM FOR INTERNATIONAL AFFAIRS

The Political Ripple Effect of 9/11

"Should national security outweigh human security?"

by Dren Maloku
Written while studying at the University of British Columbia

Abstract

This paper will first assess the variation in policy between Canada's liberal and Australia's restrictionist border control policies (BCPs) as they have unfolded since 9/11, demonstrating the heightening issue of national security. The paper will then examine the divergence in the BCPs of Australia and Canada in light of the immigration theories of Jennifer Hyndman and Christian Joppke. Furthermore, the paper concentrates on contextualizing links between the externalization of asylum and national security, underlining the political importance of a statutory Bill of Rights in relation to the variations in BCPs. Finally, this paper will conclude that multicultural states such as Australia and Canada should strive towards striking a balance between national security and human security while extending the scope of their safety measures to also integrate multicultural inclusiveness.

> It would be a mistake to treat human rights as though there
> were a trade-off to be made between human rights and goals
> such a security and development... [S]trategies based on
> the protection of human rights are vital both for our moral
> standing and the practical effectiveness of our actions.[1]

– Former United Nations Secretary General Kofi Annan

While no Western state ought to expel its own citizens, it is the sovereign legal prerogative of a Western state to regulate the present inflow of asylum seekers within its sovereign borders. In the wake of the 9/11 terrorist attacks, many Western states responded with a crackdown on movement along their borders. They also added new security policies. These included contested measures such as registration requirements for non-citizens and heightened scrutiny for potential asylum claimants.[2] The increased security at borders aimed—through preventing alleged terrorists, traffickers and human smugglers from entering borders and exploiting the refugee system—to primarily reinforce two notions: to protect national security and restore the confidence of the nation.

Indeed, Western scholars agree that their respective societies tend to emphasize having autonomy, self-sufficiency and independence. This was done even though it was after 9/11 when it was made clear that terrorism caused a major shift in political discourse. Before it was human security. Now it was national security.

Nevertheless, one could argue that the securitization of asylum is neither a viable nor a suitable solution to the surreal issue of forced displacement and irregular immigration.[3] As a preliminary remark, it should be noted that the term asylum seeker used in this paper is employed by countries to refer to "illegal migrants." These people are oftentimes referred to as "boat people," "refugees," and so on.

This paper first assesses the variation in policy between Canada's liberal and Australia's restrictive border control policies (BCPs) as they have unfolded since 9/11, demonstrating the heightening issue of national security. The paper will then examine the divergence in the BCPs of Australia and Canada in light of the immigration theories of Jennifer Hyndman and Christian Joppke. Furthermore, this paper concentrates on contextualizing links between the externalization of asylum and national security, underlining the political importance of a statutory Bill of Rights in relation to the variations in BCPs. Finally, this paper will conclude that multicultural states such as Australia and Canada should strive towards striking a balance between national security and human security while extending the scope of their safety measures to also integrate multicultural inclusivity.

By definition, almost all asylum seekers, under the Refugee Convention (RC) of 1951 are "presumed to be refugees" until proven "otherwise." [4] However, in the post 9/11 era, the process of asylum, according to Hyndman was "...increasingly characterized as a security issue[,] rather than one of protection for refugees ensconced in international law."[5] Particularly, international politics experienced a major shift in its development at a core level; it went from having flexible norms within its legal framework towards having more politicized practices.[6] While no explicit classifications that link foreign nationals to terrorists exist, the inference that connects these two groups is evident and very much indulged in discussions that pertain to the subject of national security.[7] Post 9/11, many western states employed extra-legal powers in order to defuse the rule of law for the singular purpose of increasing preemptive security measures in order to protect the interest of national security.[8] The political ripple effect of the 9/11 attacks pressured the Canadian government to recognize the need to implement tighter BCPs; however, despite 9/11 the Canadian government believed that the importance of the freedom of movement and that of due process both guaranteed under the 1982 Charter of Rights and Freedoms should be emphasized over the importance of securitization. Conversely, the absence of a Bill of Rights made it possible for the Australian government to implement tighter BCPs that would not only securitize the border but would also securitize asylum with the primary goal of reducing the number of refugee claimants and asylum seekers at the border.

However, when it comes to BCPs one knows that the power of the western states is not limitless. The international community is governed by international laws and conventions such as the 1951 RC Convention and the 1982 United Nations Convention on the Law of the Sea (UNCLOS), all of which bind nation-states to adhere and oblige to international legal obligations.[9] Failure to do so will result in sanctions or even in the use of the military force.[10] The 1951 RC and the 1967 Protocol, which both Australia and Canada have endorsed, place some restrictions on when and how states ought to exercise their border control powers. Article 33 of the 1951 RC declares that "...[n]o Contracting State shall expel or return ('refouler') a refugee in any manner whatsoever to the frontiers of territories where his life or freedom would be threatened on account of his race, religion, nationality, membership of a particular social group or political opinion."[11] Nevertheless, despite all legal conformities that countries have to abide, one might wonder under what conditions can immigrant-receiving countries such as Australia and Canada refuse to grant refugee status solely based on national security grounds, even though the asylum seekers prior to applying have already met the 1951 RC provisions?

The Australian Borders Control Policies Post 9/11

The Australian government may argue that their BCPs follow and comply with the obligations of the 1951 RC and the 1967 Protocol but post 9/11, access to the rights and safeguards enshrined therein, particularly for asylum seekers, have been increasingly limited to say the least.[12] This section of the paper will analyze how the restrictive BCPs of Australia failed to balance national security with the need to protect its citizens against the threat of terrorism and instead employed extra-legal geographies which aimed at excluding asylum seekers at all costs from reaching their sovereign shores and making a refugee claim.[13]

The Australian Prime Minister John Howard condemned the 9/11 attacks by labeling them as a direct attack on the core values and principles and essentially On the Way of Life of Western nations.[14] Hence, Elisabeth Porter asserts that what united Australians in the 2001 federal elections was the need to elect a strong leadership that would be tough on illegal undocumented aliens and would support the protection of Australian borders from illegal intruders.[15] Since the early 2000's, Australia has constructed aggressive BCPs that deter illegal and undocumented migrants from landing in its shores and filing refugee claims. These BCPs dictate that individuals who did not have a visa and arrived at the shores of Australia, regardless if they were going to file an asylum claim or not, were immediately to be imprisoned in detention camps or expelled out of the border until their case was processed.[16] In August 2001, the Norwegian cargo ship MV Tampa rescued 433 migrants escaping war-torn Afghanistan from the Indonesian vessel

Palapa off the shores of Christmas Island in Australia.[17] The Australian government refused permission to the Norwegian vessel to access its territory and this incident, which came to be known as the Tampa incident, resulted in a standoff.[18] The Australian government's hardline stance on BCPs during the Tampa affair marked the beginning of tougher BCPs aimed at deterring future asylum seekers and led to what is now known the Pacific Solution.[19] Under the Pacific Solution, some hundred smaller islands such as Christmas Island, Ashmore Reef and the Cocos Islands were "excised" from the purview of the 1958 Migration Act ("MA") and asylum seekers could no longer afford the opportunity to access Australian courts.[20] Furthermore, the Pacific Solution granted unprecedented powers to the Australian Navy to seize and ship arriving boat people for detention and formal processing off to detention camps located on the small islands. [21]

In retrospect, "mandatory detention" was introduced in 1992 in order to deal appropriately with illegal and undocumented migrants.[22] Meanwhile, after the Tampa incident, the mandatory detention strategy contributed towards "legitimizing the de-humanization" of asylum and towards creating a two-tier system of immigration; one for the legal and one for illegal migrants.[23] Mandatory detention was now implemented in order to deter asylum seekers from claiming refugee status.[24] Asylum seekers who were apprehended at the border were then placed in remote detentions centers such as Wommera, Baxter and Nauru.[25] Poor human rights conditions soon followed with many young children and pregnant women being detained with no right to basic health care.[26] Ghassan Hage described this system as "ethnic caging," which divided ""Australians from the "non-Australians."[27] At the same time, senior Australian politicians fostered "... people's fear of terrorist threats by promoting the idea that the mainly Afghani and Iraqi asylum-seekers might be criminals, terrorists and morally shallow people who do shocking things like throw their children into the sea."[28] Although there is no evidence in Porter's article that renders any truth in the alleged malicious behavior of Muslim asylum seekers, comments of this nature still managed to surface in Australian society. Porter affirms that within some of the immigration laws that exist in Australia there is an "... associative logic of racism at work ... whereby ...claims about asylum-seekers are attached to Arab-Australians and Muslims in general."[29]

Ironically, terrorism became synonymously associated with asylum and Australian BCPs with protection of Australia's national defense.[30] Accordingly, the Australian government put the interest of national security over that of human security and many asylum seekers were scrutinized as a result.[31] The government justified the exclusion of these asylum seekers from the rest of the Australian society under the banner of "regional insecurity."[32] Like Porter, Hyndman's theory also asserts that a shift in emphasis from legal towards political discourses in asylum practices occurred here and Australia has resorted to the use of the political domain in order to exclude asylum seekers from their sovereign territory where they could claim refugee status.[33] Furthermore, Hyndman reasons that this shift has created a political vacuum, which has allowed Australia to operate within its extra-jurisdictional provisions and strip stateless individuals of their refugee rights while externalizing asylum.[34] Already repressed through the use of detention, the Pacific Solution and tough BCPs, asylum seekers who were on the move were now also denied protection under the judicial system in Australia because of the politics of exclusion.[35] The Australian government utilized the practices of legislative excision to exclude and deter boats that carry asylum seekers from reaching its sovereign shores.[36] Simultaneously, the absence of a Bill of Rights contributed implicitly in the creation of detention camps and in the implementation of Draconian BCPs that not only were ineffective but also infringed upon the provisions of many international treaties Australia endorsed.

Legal scholar George Williams in his book The Case for an Australian Bill of Rights, argues that 9/11, the issue of the Tampa affair and the existence of the mandatory detention camps only strengthen the case for the amendment on an Australian Bill of Rights.[37] Australia is the only Western country that lacks a Bill of Rights.[38] Thus, Williams asserts that an Australian Bill of Rights is imperative in facilitating the basic right to asylum seekers and in balancing national security against individual liberties and democratic values.[39] In its absence, the High Court of Australia ("HCA") is forced to resort to the MA of 1958 and to international laws and human conventions in order to deal with human rights issues.[40] The absence of a written or unwritten constitutional bill hinders the HCA from assessing the changes against human rights principles in a post 9/11 context. Therefore post 9/11 there are two components that have shaped Australia's restrictionist attitude towards border control. First, Australia's geo-political location surrounded by developing nations and third world countries has made it an easier target for illegal migration to occur. Second, the absence of such an important legal check such as the Bill of Rights allows Australia's BCPs to restrict the rights of asylum to foreign migrants more than its equivalent counterpart Canada.[41]

1st Rival Theory

Aforementioned proximity to Third World countries has created a tension in Australia regarding migration and human trafficking. A rival theory asserts that the restrictionist public opinion on social issues in Australia has resulted in the implementation of these BCPs. Australians support stricter border policies that deter the acceptance of foreign citizens, asylum seekers and refugees because they disapprove of their "illegal" means of transportation. In other words, they suspect human trafficking is involved in cross-border movements. Arguably, during the Tampa Incident "boat people" had hired "human traffickers" to smuggle them from Indonesia into the shores of Australia.[42]

While this is a possible explanation to consider, this rival theory is problematic for a number of reasons. Firstly, there seems to be a misconception in the labeling of the action that confuses "human trafficking" with "human smuggling," which needs to be addressed before we move any further.[43] In his article "Snakeheads and Smuggling," Patrick R. Keefer gives a clear distinction of what human smuggling is and how it is different from human trafficking. Human trafficking, Keefer argues, involves the transportation of persons from one destination to another either against their will or under some fictitious grounds.[44] Human smuggling, however, is a contract-based operation, which depends upon the corresponding agreement between the willing party and the human smuggler.[45] Moreover, human smugglers are not forcing their clients to take the journey, unlike many human traffickers who force their victims into the sex trade or manual labor in inhumane conditions. As such, instances of human smugglers doing something of this nature are extremely rare, since their focus is the completion of the "business transaction." [46] Fredrich Heckmann argues that most of the cross-border illegal immigration nowadays is undertaken with the help of human smugglers.[47] There are many other aspects of Heckmann's article that are relevant to this particular topic of BCPs; however, this paper will not address them in depth. In short, Heckmann's theory is very critical of rival theories that support mafia-type organizations and human trafficking to be the main agents involved in cross-border movement.[48] Moreover, he discredits theories as such and demonstrates empirically that no possible connection exists between human smuggling and the smuggling of illegal drugs and weapons.[49]

The Canadian Border Control Policies Post 9/11

Although Canada, in the aftermath of 9/11, witnessed a great deal of "alteration in the field of law", there were few "alterations in practice."[50] This section of the paper will analyze the liberal BCPs of Canada and demonstrate how they vary from the BCPs of Australia in the post-9/11 contexts. Post 9/11, Australia witnessed the detention of approximately 2,000 individuals under the suspicion that they were terrorists, in contrast to Canada whose numbers of alleged detainees could "be counted on the fingers of one hand."[51] What is the cause of this policy variance?

The reason why Canada's BCPs differ from those of Australia is primarily because Canada's BCPs abide by the Charter. The Charter, in a sense, restrains the Canadian government from imposing stricter BCPs that do not conform to the provisions of the Charter. Christian Joppke asserts that aside from the influence of client politics in liberal states, an important component that is quite often over-looked, is the legal process component.[52] Furthermore, he affirms that the legal process in liberal countries is an important source that influences the domestic BCPs.[53] Joppke argues that the capacity of Western liberal countries to control their border policies has increased; however, due to the presence of domestic laws and legislatures, some countries are "self- restrained" and "internally hindered" from utilizing the full capacity of strict BCPs.[54] He reasons that the policy varia-tion between various liberal countries comes as a result of the legal process, the role of the courts and the existence of a Bill of Rights. Now drawing upon Jop-pke's assertions, one could argue that what drives Canada's liberal BCPs to differ from those of Australia is precisely the existence of these three legal components. Hence, the judicial system in Canada played an instrumental role in facilitating the transition of these anti-terrorism legislations into domestic law. Since it's all too easy to confuse the perpetrators with the victims of the terror, the courts in Canada ensured that the meaning of terrorism does not interfere with refugee law and with BCPs, a process the HCA failed to exhibit.[55]

Two pieces of legislation, which were instrumental in setting up, the agenda of national security in Canada post 9/11 were: The Immigration and Refugee Protection Act ("IRPA") and the Anti Terrorist Act ("ATA").[56] The former proposed to be tough on external threats and on human smuggling, whereas the latter was concerned with terrorism and terrorist groups and their activities.[57] Nevertheless, both of these acts were formulated in conformity with Canada's long tradition in human rights and the provisions of the Charter.[58] Furthermore, in order to improve its lenient stance on BCPs, Canada, on the advice of the United States, decided to join forces with the U.S. in a new security accord called the Smart Border Agreement ("SBA") that aimed to strengthen BCPs, enhancing the screening process and fostering cooperation between the two countries.[59] However, even when agreements such as the SBA or laws such as IRPA were amended and implemented in BCPs the judicial system in Canada, due to the existence of the Charter, would have the ability to strike down different provisions of the agreement or the act entirely if their provisions violated the clauses of the Charter.

Canadian courts differ from the Australian courts in that they can afford to offer, under the provisions of the Charter, the right to liberty, due process and a fair hearing even to those who enter the country illegally.[60] In 2006, the Supreme Court of Canada ("SCC") heard the arguments presented in three different security certificate cases, which were all later joined to the common appeal of Charkaoui v. Canada.[61] Mr. Charkaoui was a permanent resident while the other two detainees where foreign nationals, all of whom were detained on various provisions of IRPA.[62] IRPA allowed the Minister of Citizenship and Immigration to issue so-called "security certificate" in rendering the detainees inadmissible to Canada on grounds of security.[63] The issue before the SCC was whether a non-criminal legislation could be used to prosecute criminal offences. The SCC stated that Canadian law does not allow "indefinite administrative detention," and demonstrated that in this instance Canada cannot use immigration laws to prosecute criminal acts.[64] Furthermore, the SCC found that the dentition of these individuals infringes on Section 7 and Section 9 of the Charter. Section 7 protects the right to life, liberty, security and due process.[65] In addition, Section 9 protects from "arbitrary detention" and the habeas corpus.[66] The SCC asserted that the detained individuals must be "accorded meaningful opportunities" to challenge the conditions of their detention or the conditions of their release.[67] As a remedy, the SCC declared "...judicial confirmation of certificates and review of detention to be of no force and effect", removing articles 33 and 77-85 from IRPA while suspending the ruling for one year.[68] The importance of the legal process in this case proved triumphant because the Canadian government was able to pass legislation that was not in conformity with the provisions of the Charter. Due to the existence of this legislation, the judges were able to adjudicate the case in favor of the foreign nationals, something that is yet to be replicated in the Australian judicial system.

One would argue that Australia's recent aggressive BCPs have been "extraordinarily inventive in circumventing the single strongest norm of the international human rights regime, the non-refoulment obligation." [69] Even though the 1951 RC and the 1967 Protocol prohibit both the expulsion on racial grounds and the refoulement of the individual who fears political persecution, the Australian government still carried on with their expulsion and refoulement policies as usual.[70] One of the possible explanations for why Australia has been able to operate within the loopholes of international law is the absence of an enforcement mechanism within international law that penalizes violating countries. Thus, the policy variation in this paper reveals that Canada BCPs domestically, unlike Australia's, are bound not only by international law but also by the power of the Charter, to oblige and protect the rights of not only Canadian citizens but also foreign nationals.[71] Hence, I argue that the legal process is crucial to explaining what the divergence in BCPs is between Australia and Canada in explaining why Canada's BCPs, even post 9/11, continued to be liberal and permitted the entrance of many other asylum seekers such as is the case with the latest Tamil boat arrivals in British Columbia in 2009 and 2010.[72]

2nd Rival Theory

An aforementioned misconception that portrays asylum seekers as welfare-scroungers has created a tension in Canada regarding public opinion to illegal migration. A rival theory asserts that the restrictionist public opinion on social issues in Canada has resulted in the implementation of stricter BCPs. Canadians have not accepted the high intake of illegal migrants through the border because they perceive them to be a burden on the Canadian economy. Agents of the Canada Border Service Agency (CBSA) believe that tougher policy control measures need to be put in place to deter the large influx of illegal migrants from entering Canada taking away Canadian jobs, among other concerns.[73]

While this is a possible explanation to consider, this rival theory is problematic for a number of reasons. Firstly, there seems to be a misconception that most of the asylum seekers in Canada are granted the right to "paid employment" through work permits while their cases are processed (CCR). In "The Economic Experiences of Refugees in Canada," Don DeVoretz concludes that refugees,like asylum seekers, are not and shall not be examined based on the total of their potential contribution to the Canadian economy.[74] Secondly, his research and data show that, despite the element of potential contribution, asylum seekers do not constitute a major drain on the Canadian economy.[75] Thirdly, if one factors that a portion of those whose claims for asylum were granted will annually start to pay taxes to the Canadian government and will not receive any government benefits, one can judge that in the end it is a clear net intake for the Canadian government and that the economic-drain hypothesis is nothing more than a common misconception.[76] Therefore, the prime moving force behind the stricter border policies in the post 9/11 Canada is not an issue of welfare-scroungers but the securitization of border and the protection of national security.

Conclusion

The tentative policy conclusion of this paper is that post 9/11 there is a divergence in the BCPs between Australia and Canada. Although both countries appear to be attempting a balance between the need to protect the rights of their own citizens and the need to combat the threat of terrorism, Canada seems to be far more progressed in this aspect as a result of the Charter. However, in the case of both countries, tightening BCPs could be somewhat counterintuitive to promoting multicultural tolerance and inclusiveness within one's own borders. One would argue that the new BCPs have little to do with preventing terrorism and more to do with controlling and regulating the refugee system. While modifying national security measures to target terrorists is not particularly new, modifying national BCPs to deliberately target the exclusion of asylum seekers under the banner of security is definitely a new occurrence that warrants more attention given its increasing commonplace practice.[77] Thus, an inclusive society, Porter argues, ought to accept the "...responsibility to protect the dignity of citizens and those seeking asylum, and [to provide] the conditions through which everyone living within its borders can flourish peacefully." [78]

Endnotes

1. In Large Freedom: Towards Development, Security and Human Rights for All 140. U.N. A/59 (2005) (Report of the Secretary-General) (quoting 1) (Kofi, Annan Commentaries).

2. Catherine, Dauvergne. "Security and Migration Law In The Less Brave New World." Sage Publications. 16, no. 533 (Spring 2007), p 543.

3. Elisabeth, Porter. "Security and Inclusiveness: Protecting Australia's Way of Life." The Peace Studies Journals. 3, no. 120 (Summer 2003), p 2.

4. Office of The High Commission for Human Rights (OHCHR). "Expulsions of aliens in international human rights law." U.N. Discussion Paper. 1, (Fall 2006), p 2.

5. Jennifer, Hyndman & Alison Mountz. "Another Brick in the Wall? Neo-Refoulement and the Externalization of Asylum by Australia and Europe." Blackwell Publishing. 43, no. 2 (Winter 2008), p 250.

6. Ibid.

7. Erin, Krueger, et al., "CANADA AFTER 9/11: NEW SECURITY MEASURES AND 'PREFERRED' IMMIGRANTS." Metropolis. no. WP09-04 (Fall 2004), p 8.

8. Hyndman, "Another Brick in the Wall? Neo-Refoulement and the Externalization of Asylum by Australia and Europe", p.250.

9. Peter, D. Fox. "International Asylum and Boat People: The Tampa Affair and Australia's Pacific Solution." Maryland Journal of International Law. 1, (Spring 2010), p. 359-60.

10. Ibid., 359.

11. Ibid., 361-2; See Also United Nations High Commissioner for Refugees. Convention and Protocol relating to the Status of Refugees. Article 33 (Refoulement definition),p. 30-32.

12. Hyndman, "Another Brick in the Wall? Neo-Refoulement and the Externalization of Asylum by Australia and Europe", p.19.

13. Ibid., 8.

14. Porter, "Security and Inclusiveness: Protecting Australia's Way of Life", p 3.

15. Ibid.

16. Hyndman, "Another Brick in the Wall? ...", p.257.

17. Fox, "International Asylum and Boat People: The Tampa Affair and Australia's Pacific Solution", p. 356.

18. Ibid., 357.

19. Ibid., 359.

20. Ibid.

21. Ibid.

22. Porter, "Security and Inclusiveness: Protecting Australia's Way of Life", p 6.

23. Ibid.

24. Ibid.

25. Hyndman, "Another Brick in the Wall? ...", p.259.

26. Porter, "Security and Inclusiveness: Protecting Australia's Way of Life", p 6.

27. Ghassan, Hage.– White nation: fantasies of white supremacy in a multicultural society (New York: Rutledge, 1998), p. 105-6.

28. Porter, "Security and Inclusiveness: Protecting Australia's Way of Life", p 5.

29. Ibid.

30. Ibid.

31. Ibid., 6.

32. Hyndman, "Another Brick in the Wall? ...", p.251-3.

33. Ibid., 251-252.

34. Ibid., 252-253.

35. Ibid., 259.

36. Ibid., 260.

37. George, Williams.– The Case for an Australian Bill of Rights: Freedom in the War on Terror (New South Wales: New South Wales UP, 2004), p. 7.

38. Ibid., 11.

39. Ibid.

40. Ibid., 16.

41. Ibid., See also 11-37.

42. Fox, "International Asylum and Boat People: ...", p. 357.

43. Patrick, Radden Keefe. "Snakeheads and Smuggling The Dynamics of Illegal Chinese Immigration." World Policy Journals. 26, No.33 (Summer 2009), p. 37.

44. Ibid.

45. Ibid.

46. Ibid.

47. Friedrich, Heckmann. "Illegal Migration: What Can We Know And What Can We Explain? The Case of Germany." European Forum for Migration Studies. 3, No.38 (Summer 2004), p. 1103.

48. Ibid.

49. Ibid., 1122.

50. Howard, Adelman. "Canadian Borders Post 9/11 and Immigration." Center for Migration Studies New York. 1, No.36 (Spring 2002), p. 19.

51. Ibid.

52. Christian, Joppke. "Why Liberal States Accept Unwanted Immigration." Cambridge University Press. 50, No.2 (Winter 1998), p. 270.

53. Ibid.

54. Ibid.

55. Asha, Kaushal and Catherine Dauvergne. "The Growing Culture of Exclusion: Trends in Canadian Refugee Exclusions." Metropolis. 6, No.11 (Summer 2011), p. 25.

56. Krueger, et al., "CANADA AFTER 9/11: NEW SECURITY MEASURES AND 'PREFERRED' IMMIGRANTS," p.7.

57. Ibid.

58. Ibid.

59. Ibid., 9.

60. Singh v. Minister of Employment and Immigration, 1 S.C.R. 177 (SCC.1985) (Opinion of the Court) (quoting 1) (Dickson C.J. Commentaries) p.61-63.

61. Charkaoui v. Canada, 1 S.C.R. 350, (SCC.9 2007) (Opinion of the Court) (quoting 1) (McLachlin C.J. Commentaries) p.1.

62. Ibid., 5.

63. Ibid.

64. Ibid; See Also Dauvergne, "Security and Migration Law In The Less Brave New World", p 539.

65. Charkaoui v. Canada, 1 S.C.R. 350, p.9.

66. Ibid., 11.

67. Ibid., 9.

68. Ibid., 77-85.

69. Joppke, "Why Liberal States Accept Unwanted Immigration", p. 269.

70. Ibid., 268.

71. Ibid; See Also Singh v. Minister of Employment and Immigration, 1 S.C.R. 177. (All).

72. Joppke, "Why Liberal States Accept Unwanted Immigration", p. 271; See Also Footnotes at the bottom in regards to MV Sun, Kaushal, "The Growing Culture of Exclusion: Trends in Canadian Refugee Exclusions", p. 23.

73. Tom, Godfrey. "Canadian economy draws illegal migrants" CN News.(Fall 2010), n.p.

74. Don, DeVoretz et al., "The Economic Experiences of Refugees in Canada." Discussion Paper. No.1088 (Spring 2004), p. 30.

75. Ibid.

76. Laura, Stempmorlok. "Why as Canadians we can't turn away Tamil ships (or any others)." Third Wave Style World Press. (Summer 2010), n.p.

77. Hyndman, "Another Brick in the Wall? ...", p.250.

78. Porter, "Security and Inclusiveness: Protecting Australia's Way of Life", p 18.

Bibliography

Annan, Kofi, "Report of the Secretary-General: In Larger Freedom: Towards Development, Security and Human Rights for All." A/59 (2005): 140. Delivered to the General Assembly, U.N. Doc. Web. Mar 30th .2012.

Adelman, Howard. "Canadian Borders Post 9/11 and Immigration." European Forum for Migration Studies. 1, No.36 (2002): 15-28. Journal Storage. Mar 30th .2012.

Charkaoui v. Canada. 1 S.C.R. 350, SCC.9 L. ed. 2007 (SCC.1986): 1-90.

Dauvergne, Catherine. "Security and Migration Law In The Less Brave New World." Social Legal Studies, 16, No.533 (2007): 533-550. Sage Publications. Mar 30th. 2012.

DeVoretz, Don, et al., "The Economic Experiences of Refugees in Canada." Discussion Paper. No.1088 (2004): 1-32. Journal Storage. Mar 30th .2012.

Erin, Krueger, et al., "Canada After 9/11: New Security Measures And 'Preferred' immigrants." Prairie Centre of Excellence for Research on Immigration andIntegration, No.9 (2004): 1-22. Metropolis. Mar 30th .2012.

Fox, D. Peter. "International Asylum and Boat People: The Tampa Affair and Australia's Pacific Solution." Maryland Journal of International Law, 1, No.1 (2010): 356- 373. Journal Storage. Mar 30th .2012.

Godfrey ,Tom. "Canadian economy draws illegal migrants" CN News. (2010): n.p. Web. Mar 30th .2012.

Hage, Ghassan. White nation: fantasies of white supremacy in a multicultural society. New York: Rutledge. 1998. Print.

Heckmann, Friedrich. "Illegal Migration: What Can We Know And What Can We Explain? The Case of Germany." European Forum for Migration Studies. 3, No.38 (2004): 1103-1135. Journal Storage. Mar 30th .2012.

Hyndman, Jennifer., and Alison Mountz. "Another Brick in the Wall? Neo-Refoulement and the Externalization of Asylum by Australia and Europe." Government and Opposition Ltd, 43, No.2 (2008): 1-18. Blackwell Publishing. Mar 30th .2012.

Joppke, Christian. "Why Liberal States Accept Unwanted Immigration." Cambridge University Press. 50, No.2 (1998): 266-293. Journal Storage. Mar 30th .2012.

Kaushal, Asha., and Catherine Dauvergne. "The Growing Culture of Exclusion: Trends in Canadian Refugee Exclusions." Metropolis. 6, No.11 (2011): 1-56. Journal Storage. Mar 30th .2012.

Keefe, Patrick, Radden. "Snakeheads and Smuggling The Dynamics of Illegal Chinese Immigration." World Policy Journal, 26, No.33 (2009): 33-44. Journal Storage. Mar 30th .2012.

Singh v. Minister of Employment and Immigration, 1 S.C.R. 177 L.ed. (SCC.1985) : 1-75.

Stempmorlok, Laura. "Why as Canadians we can't turn away Tamil ships (or any others)." Third Wave Style World Press. (2010): n.p. Web. Mar 30th .2012.

OHCHR. Expulsions of aliens in international human rights law." U.N. Discussion Paper, 1, No.1 (2006): 1-19. United Nations. Mar 30th .2012.

Porter, Elisabeth. "Security and Inclusiveness: Protecting Australia's Way of Life." Peace. Conflict and Development, 3, No.120 (2003): 1-18. Southern Cross UP. Mar 30th .2012.

UNHCR. "United Nations High Commissioner for Refugees. Convention and Protocol relating to the Status of Refugees." U.N. Publication, 1, No.1 (2011): 1-56. United Nations. Mar 30th .2012.

Williams, George The Case for an Australian Bill of Rights: Freedom in the War on Terror. New South Wales: New South Wales UP. 2004. Print.

The Obama Doctrine

On the United States' consistently realist approach to democratization in the face of the Arab Spring.

by Konstantin Sietzy
Written while studying at the London School of Economics

Abstract

Following the Arab Spring in the summer of 2012, critics of President Barack Obama asserted his response to the burgeoning unrest in the Middle East was troublingly inconsistent. This paper draws on the opposite conclusion, arguing instead that the United States adopted a realist approach and consistently sought democratization and regime change in nations affected by the Arab Spring.

Introduction

Non-involvement in Tunisia; strong calls for change in Egypt; military interven-tion in Libya to save lives; denying such intervention in Syria; keeping silent on the Gulf States: the fact that US reactions to the Arab Awakening have differed for every single affected country has led to allegations of inconsistency. Human-itarians deplore tolerating slaughter in Syria (Roth, 2012). Sovereigntists attack interference in domestic affairs (The Daily Star, 2012). Cynics point to differing deposits of oil (Xinyi, 2011). Nonetheless, it can be argued that US foreign policy towards the Arab Spring has been consistent: in every instance, the US aimed for democratization and regime change (albeit with minimal resource commitment) as long as this was in accordance with realist considerations. In this sense, the Arab Spring saw a doctrinaire, undeviating application of what can be described as the 'Obama Doctrine.'

The first part of this essay will explain why a consistent Obama Doctrine indeed exists and how it is composed. The second part of the essay addresses the most pertinent examples: Egypt and Libya as clear examples of the US backing regime change, and the ostensible exception Syria, turning out to prove the rule that realist considerations underlie each intervention.

The Obama Doctrine

The Obama doctrine is the combination of two seemingly antithetical impulses: a fundamentally realist outlook on policy, domestic and foreign; and the con-comitant belief in the importance of soft power and the Roosevelt approach of being a "Good Neighbor," (Walser, 2012) on a global scale. The realist strand in Obama's foreign policy stems from a consciousness of limited American resourc-es (Obama, "Libya", 2011), summarized in "two unspoken beliefs: that the relative power of the U.S. is declining, as rivals like China rise, and that the U.S. is reviled in many parts of the world." (Lizza, 2011) Prudently, Obama realizes that the lat-ter component is not an abstract but a practical threat to American security. On September 23rd 2009 he addressed the United Nations conceding: "I took office at a time when many around the world had come to view America with skepticism and distrust ... and this has fed an almost reflexive anti-Americanism." (Obama, 2009) Thus the second impetus behind the Obama Doctrine is a desire to better the American image in the world (Brower, 2012). The centrality of the Arab world in this mission was proven months earlier when on June 4th Obama unprecedentedly embraced Islam's importance in his Cairo-speech, "specifically trying to undo the damage that he thought George W. Bush had done to the US in the Middle East." (Dodge, 2012)

The product of the need to reconcile these two drives is the Obama Doctrine: acting in the international community as part of multilateral initiatives and in accordance with international law. Obama's UN speech heralded an "era of collective engagement" and expressed American willingness for cooperation (Obama, 2009); yet realism was never far so that Obama defended cooperation in Libya domestically in terms of "allies and partners ... [bearing] their share of the burden and [paying] their share of the costs." (Obama, "Libya", 2011)

The Context

The balance-act between supporting democratization and hedging bets in the Arab Spring was largely due to, and reflected in, divisions in Obama's administration. Idealistic support for democratization was infused by Obama's "warrior women" Hillary Clinton, Samantha Power and Susan Rice, driven by each of their memories of the failure to stop genocide in Rwanda (Dreyfuss, 2012). The crucial determinant of Obama's attitude towards the Arab Spring was his memorandum entitled "Political Reform in the Middle East and North Africa," sent to foreign policy advisers in August 2010, creating a task group to review US policy through "'country by country' strategies on political reform" in face of simmering popular discontent. Its findings pointed towards political reform, claiming that tolerating autocrats to ensure political stability was no longer in America's practical interest (Lizza, 2011)[1]. The administration's ideological desire for democratization no longer automatically stood in conflict with realist perspectives on the Middle East.

Egypt

Following seven days of rebellion, on February 1st 2011 Obama demanded, "an orderly transition [that] must be meaningful, it must be peaceful, and it must begin now." (Obama, "Egypt", 2011) The historical US position of supporting auto-

---

[1] Importantly, oil-security is a different justification from political stability; thus the Gulf monarchies were not necessarily included in this strategic review. This omission explains the absence of Bahrain in this essay.

crats in favor of stability was no longer deemed necessary (see above); and the specific case of supporting Mubarak against a young, democratic w Muslim (although largely secular) opposition actively endangered the US project of garnering respect in the Muslim world. In the words of Ryan Lizza (2011), "it's always a good idea, politically, to support brave young men and women risking their lives for freedom, especially when their opponent is an eighty-two-year old dictator with Swiss bank accounts." Yet the need to "assure other autocratic allies that the U.S. did not hastily abandon its friends" precluded abandoning Mubarak too quickly and overtly (Lizza, 2011), explaining Obama's equivocal choice of words.

Indeed, for a number of reasons stronger interference in the Egyptian case was not feasible. In a negative sense, the limited level of violence gave no basis for an intervention on the grounds of RtoP and would thus have lacked international legitimacy, fundamentally countering the Obama Doctrine approach. In a positive sense, it seemed unnecessary. A regime wavering between confrontation and concessions (Shehata, 2011) implied a not unwaveringly intransigent dictator. Obama was inclined to support reform over radical change, as Mubarak relinquishing power would have constitutionally demanded elections within 60 days, a period which analysts predicted would give liberal moderates no chance to organize against the Muslim Brotherhood (Lizza, 2011) (this scenario of threat betraying that not even Obama can rid himself of certain prejudiced concerns). Secondly, clandestine support for change seemed propitious given divisions in the regime between military and civilian elements (Shehata, 2011). Indeed, allegations have surfaced that indirect US pressure on CENTCOM-trained Egyptian military officers may have played a role in the eventual coup (Dodge, 2012).

Thus the US position towards Egypt was in clear line with the Obama Doctrine: a lack of international consensus against Mubarak was sufficient to prevent open calls for regime change – and this option was possible because stronger intervention was not even deemed necessary. US policy stayed within both the limits of the possible and the necessary to achieve the democratization that had become the new policy objective.

Libya

While Lizza (2011) identifies "intervention in Libya" as "an unusually clear choice between interests and values," US foreign policy was again driven by realist cost-benefit analyses. Not inconsistency, but the combination of greater necessity and greater possibility determined the contrasting magnitude of US intervention between Egypt and Libya. Necessity stemmed from urgency: on March 16th Gadhafi's forces bore down on Benghazi declaring unambiguously: "It's over. We are coming tonight. We will find you in your closets" (Lizza, 2011). US supreme military power defines that it is generally held accountable for the "actions or inactions" of the international community; in the case of a massacre in Benghazi, "no one would have blamed Berlin or Brasilia for that. They would have blamed Washington" (Jones, 2011: 56). The second imperative was domestic bargaining: "haunted" by memories of Rwanda and Bosnia, Power, Rice and Clinton galvanized Obama into action, winning the debate against skeptics such as then-Defense Secretary Gates and National Security Adviser Donilon.

Necessity was complemented by possibility: "We had a unique ability to stop that violence: an international mandate for action, a broad coalition prepared to join us, the support of Arab countries, and a plea for help from the Libyan people themselves. We also had the ability to stop [Gadhafi] … without putting American troops on the ground." (Obama, "Libya", 2011) Obama's summary reflects the Libyan case's accordance with his doctrine: showing the world that a UNSC decision would "support the Arab League. Not support the United States – support the Arab League" (Hillary Clinton; qtd. in Lizza, 2011), precluded allegations of American unilateralism. European allies Britain and France had strong incentives to take action (natural resources, refugee-crisis concerns, and international status considerations), were in an immediate position to do so, and were even seen to take the initiative at the UNSC (Elliott, 2011). The geography of the conflict also made intervention without committing ground troops uniquely feasible (Patrick, 2011), an absolute requirement both to achieve international and domestic consensus. Thus this chance was "as good as it gets" (Allin and Jones, 2011: 208) for the Obama Doctrine's requirements of multilateralism and not jeopardizing America's standing in the (Muslim) world, and an ideological commitment to democracy-promotion.

Syria

Syria is the exception that proves the rule. Again US foreign policy is unequivocal in its calls for regime change (Obama first demanding Assad's resignation August 18th 2011: Obama, "Syria", 2011). Yet a US military intervention has not been an option, again not reflecting inconsistency but betraying that the Obama administration's liberal ideology operates within the limits set by realist considerations. Indeed Obama had openly conceded in 2007 that the US cannot commit to the prevention of even genocide indiscriminately (Lizza, 2011); and had taken care to emphasize that Libya was "unique" (see above). Contrasting Syria with the "very viable" situation in Libya, officials are deeply sceptical about intervention in Syria (qtd. in Bohan, 2012), adducing Assad's much stronger military, a disunited opposition and the lack of clear territorial divisions (Bumiller, 2012). Secondly, intervention in Syria would defy the Obama Doctrine of multilateralism: international consensus has "evaporated" (Evans, 2012), and Russia and China directly vetoed a UNSC resolution stipulating regime change (Martinez, 2012). Criticism also comes from other BRICS and Non-western States, directly resulting from disagreement of the Western coalition's perceived overstepping of its mandate in actively ousting Gadhafi (Evans, 2012).

The absence of military intervention is complemented by the administrations vociferous condemnations of "despicable" Russian and Chinese blockade-tactics (Clinton, qtd.in Telegraph, 2012), and "Friends-of-Syria" summits (Telegraph, 2012), aiming for the moral high-ground. Thus while democratization again remains the ultimate objective, it is superseded in the short-term by the necessity to portray a committed but nevertheless lawful America, and the impracticability of military intervention.

Conclusion

This trinity of challenges to Obama's foreign policy sees a systematic continuation of what one can perceive as an Obama Doctrine: ameliorating America's image in the world by showing commitment but operating multilaterally and within the constraints of international law. While Libya was "as good as it gets," stronger intervention in Egypt and Syria came up against realist hurdles. Yet policy is always guided by the necessity to display engagement and gain the moral high ground, conscious of the need for winning the respect of those parts of the world in which America's image has been blackened.

Bibliography

Allin, Dana H. and Erik Jones. "As Good as it Gets?" Survival: Global Politics and Strategy May 2011: 205-215.

Bohan, Caren. "U.S. Deeply Skeptical About Syria Military Options." 10 Mar. 2012. Chicago Tribune Website. 11 Mar. 2012 <http://www.chicagotribune.com/news/politics/sns-rt-us-usa-syria-obamabre8290 bq-20120310,0,2990385.story>.

Brower, Kate Andersen. "Obama Says Restoring U.S. Image Abroad Was a Top Accomplishment." 16 Feb. 2012. Bloomberg. 10 Mar. 2012 <http://www.bloomberg.com/news/2012-02-16/obama-says-restoring-u-s-image-abroad-was-a-top-accomplishment.html>.

Bumiller, Elisabeth. "U.S. Defense Officials Say Obama Reviewing Military Options in Syria." 7 Mar. 2012. The New York Times Website. 11 Mar. 2012 <http://www.nytimes.com/2012/03/08/world/middleeast/united-states-defense-officials-stress-nonmilitary-options-on-syria.html?_r=1>.

Dodge, Toby. Intervention 2: The Arab Spring. London: London School of Economics, 7 Mar. 2012.

Dreyfuss, Robert. "Obama's Women Adviser Pushed War Against Libya." 19 Mar. 2011. The Nation Online. 10 Mar. 2012 <http://www.thenation.com/blog/159346/obamas-women-pushed-war-against-libya>.

Elliott, Michael. "Viewpoint: How Libya Became a French and British War." 19 Mar. 2011. Time Magazine Online. 11 Mar. 2012 <http://www.time.com/time/world/article/0,8599,2060412,00.html>.

Evans, Gareth. "Responsibility While Protecting." 27 Jan. 2012. Project Syndicate. 10 Mar. 2012 <http://www.project-syndicate.org/commentary/evans14/English>.

Jones, Bruce. "Libya and the Responsibilities of Power." Survival: Global Politics and Strategy May 2011: 51-60.

Lizza, Ryan. "The Consequentialist." 2 May 2011. The New Yorker. 13 Feb. 2012 <http://www.newyorker.com/reporting/2011/05/02/110502fa_fact_lizza?printable=true#ixzz1KWzFQym6>.

Martinez, Luis. "US 'Disgusted' by Russia, China Veto of UN Resolution to End Violence in Syria." 4 Feb. 2012. ABC News Website. 11 Mar. 2012 <http://abcnews.go.com/blogs/politics/2012/02/us-disgusted-by-russia-china-veto-of-un-resolution-to-end-violence-in-syria/>.

Obama, Barack. "Obama's Speech to the United Nations General Assembly." 23 September 2009. The New York Times Website. 10 Mar. 2012 <http://www.nytimes.com/2009/09/24/us/politics/24prexy.text.html?_r=1&pagewanted=all>.

"Obama's Statement on Syria, August 2011." 18 Aug. 2011. Council on Foreign Relations Website. 11 Mar. 2012 <http://www.cfr.org/syria/obamas-statement-syria-august-2011/p25659>.

"Remarks by the President in Address to the Nation on Libya." 28 Mar. 2011. The White House: Office of the Press Secretary Website. 10 Mar. 2012 <http://www.whitehouse.gov/the-press-office/2011/03/28/remarks-president-address-nation-libya>.

"Remarks by the President on the Situation in Egypt." 1 Feb. 2011. The White House: Office of the Press Secretary. 10 Mar. 2012 <http://www.whitehouse.gov/the-press-office/2011/02/01/remarks-president-situation-egypt>.

Patrick, Stewart. "Libya and the Future of Humanitarian Intervention." 26 Aug. 2011. Foreign Affairs Magazine Website. 2 Dec. 2011 <http://www.foreignaffairs.com/articles/68233/stewart-patrick/libya-and-the-future-of-humanitarian-intervention>.

Roth, Kenneth. "Time to Abandon the Autocrats and Embrace Rights." 2012. Human Rights Watch: World Report 2012. 11 Mar. 2012 <http://www.hrw.org/world-report-2012/time-abandon-autocrats-and-embrace-rights>.

Shehata, Dina. "The Fall of the Pharaoh: How Hosni Mubarak's Reign Came to an End." Foreign Affairs May/Jun 2011: 26-32.

The Daily Star. "Russian Envoy Says Syria's Sovereignty Priority for Moscow." 11 Feb. 2012. The Daily Star Online. 11 Mar. 2012 <http://www.dailystar.com.lb/News/Politics/2012/Feb-11/162925-russian-envoy-says-syrias-sovereignty-priority-for-moscow.ashx#axzz1oooEZPWZ>.

The Telegraph. "Syria: Hillary Clinton Calls Russia and China 'Despicable' for Opposing UN Resolution." 25 Feb. 2012. The Telegraph Website. 11 Mar. 2012 <http://www.telegraph.co.uk/news/worldnews/middleeast/syria/9105470/Syria-Hillary-Clinton-calls-Russia-and-China-despicable-for-opposing-UN-resolution.html>.

Walser, Ray. "Summit of the Americas: Return of Good Neighbour Policy?" 21 Apr. 2009. Real Clear World. 11 Mar. 2012 <http://www.realclearworld.com/articles/2009/04/fifth_summit_of_the_americas_r.html>.

Xinyi, Zhang. "Libya Intervention: Driven by Oil or Humanitarianism? ." 23 Mar. 2011. People's Daily Online. 11 Mar. 2012 <http://english.peopledaily.cn/90001/90780/91343/7329108.html>.

Debt and Power

The impact of Chinese ownership of U.S. debt and assets on Sino-American relations.

Rhiannon M. Kirkland
Written while studying at the University of Calgary

Abstract

As China continues to own more and more of the United States' debt, economic and political actors contemplate the impact it will have on Sino-American relations. This paper seeks to determine whether China's ownership of American securities will impact the two countries' strategic interactions and in what ways. Ultimately, the paper concludes China has gained significant autonomy and that the US, moving forward, will have trouble coercing the Chinese government to adopt pro-American policy. At the same time, China will be unable to coerce the United States in any meaningful ways.

Introduction

Since the beginning of Deng Xiaoping's reform and opening in the 1980s, China has experienced remarkable economic growth and is beginning to come into its own as an international economic player. Expectations for China's rise are mixed. Some argue that China's rise will be peaceful as the international system moves towards a multi-polar system, while others contend that China's rise will challenge the current hegemon, the United States, and will result in conflict (Guo and Teng, Pant, Zhao). Recently, Chinese officials have made suggestions about a move away from the dollar as the world's reserve currency. China wants a greater voice in the IMF and World Bank (Drezner 2009, 7). For many, these actions demonstrate increased Chinese assertiveness in recent years. As China becomes a bigger economic player, it subsequently wants more power in the global economy.

China has also established itself as a major international creditor, while at the same time, the United States has developed a large debt (Jensen and Weston 14). This is not the first time that the United States has been a debtor, however. Historically, the U.S. has borrowed from allied states to which it provides security guarantees (Milner 1993, 306). This is not the case with China. Many view the problem as being opposed to U.S. debt, but rather with who is purchasing it and how it may change power dynamics with them. Ferguson and Schularick observe, "Seldom in history has one great power been so invested in the bonds of another" (2007, 229). The United States cannot exercise the same power over China as it did over West Germany and does over Japan — who are and have been allied states and militarily dependent on the United States. China is a potential military rival that is responsible for its own security (Milner 316).

There is the potential for economic interdependence — manifested here in the debtor-creditor relationship — to leave China vulnerable. Prasad argues that China is dependent on "excessive consumption in the U.S. and some other advanced industrial economies" because of "a saving glut caused by inappropriate policies in China" (2009, 1). China's economic development is tied to "a stable external environment" (Medeiros 15) of which relations with the U.S. are a key element.

If China were to use American debt as a hard power asset and either refuse to acquire new debt or dump debt on the open market, there could be broader financial implications. Milner argues, "A creditor's attempt to manipulate the relationship with the debtor may carry with it the possibility of undermining its own and the world's monetary system" (536). If this were to occur, China's long-term economic health would suffer.

Some politicians and observers have suggested that American dependence on Chinese credit acts as a restraint on the ability of the United States to resist China's foreign policy advances. Benjamin Friedman writes, "because we have become a net debtor heavily dependent on foreign lenders… we will have to accept the influence and control exercised here by foreign owners" (75–76). There are concerns that China's creditor role gives China influence over important U.S. financial decisions. In December 2008, James Rickards, an adviser to U.S. Director of National Intelligence Mike McConnell, observed that China possessed defacto veto power over certain U.S. interest rate and exchange rate decisions (Drezner 2008, 8).

Chinese officials have expressed the need for favorable treatment by the U.S. as a result of ownership American debt. Gao Xiqing, the head of the China Investment Corporation (CIC) said, "I won't say kowtow, but at least, be nice to the countries that lend you money" (Drezner 8). There is the possibility that U.S. ability to pressure China on sensitive issue like currency manipulation and human rights will be reduced. During the 2008 US presidential campaign, Barack Obama said, "It's pretty hard to have a tough negotiation when the Chinese are our bankers" (Drezner 15).

Many of these statements express concern on the part of U.S. policy makers, and assertiveness on the part of the Chinese over the potential implications of American debt to China. However, once rhetoric is set aside, does China's creditor status give it power over the United States? Can financial power be converted into political power? Does this affect the security relationship between China and the United States, and if it so, how?

This paper is organized in five parts. The first examines levels of U.S. debt to China, and some of the factors contributing to Chinese accumulation of American assets. The second examines broader global imbalances that created the conditions for the Sino-American creditor-debtor relationship and the potential implications of a long-term rebalancing of these relations. The third section looks at the literature on economic and financial statecraft. The fourth section provides an analysis of international relations theory and how it applies in the context of this issue. The last section examines influence attempts by China during the financial crisis and gains in autonomy resulting from China's creditor status.

Levels of U.S. debt to China

In April 2009, China held $2.3 trillion dollars in foreign assets, of which $1.5 trillion were in U.S. assets (Ali 2012, 24 and Drezner 2008, 8). These holdings include $760 billion in United States Treasury bonds, $489 billion in Bonds issued by Fannie Mae, Freddie Mac, Ginnie Mae and the Federal Home Loan Bank, $121 billion in American corporate bonds, $104 billion in United States equities, and $41 billion in deposits (Ali 24 and Setser and Pandey 3). Fergusson and Schularick write, "Over the past five years, China's reserves increased by almost $200 billion a year and by August 2007 were equivalent to more than 40 per cent of the country's GDP. The figure of $200 billion also comes close to the amount of net new issuance of U.S. treasury securities and agency debt: $200 billion in 2005 and $195 billion in 2005" (229). However, China's true portfolio is likely larger than what has been disclosed (Setser and Pandey 3).

China holds 11 percent of all outstanding treasury debt and about 20 percent of all foreign held United States government debt (Fergusson and Schularick 2007, 229). Morrison and Labonte write, "U.S. Treasury securities are issued to finance the federal budget deficit. Of public debt that is privately held, about half is held by foreigners" (2). In September 2008, China surpassed Japan as the largest holder of United States debt (Drezner 2009, 8). China now has twice as many holdings of U.S. debt and securities as Japan and four times that of Russia and Saudi Arabia (Drezner 13). This debt is created through treasury bonds, which are the means through which all governments borrow cash. The U.S. government issues treasury bonds and other states, individuals and institutions buy it (Rogers 2012).

While the United States' debt may be large in absolute terms, it is small compared to that of other states. In 2005, the U.S. debt was 65 per cent of its GDP, while it was 158 percent for Japan and 109 percent for Italy (Milner 306). China's bilateral trade surplus rose from $84 billion in 2000 to $266 billion in 2008 — equivalent to 1.9 percent of U.S. GDP. The share of China's exports going to the

U.S. declined from 22 percent in 2000 to 19 percent in 2008 — about the same level as the E.U. (Prasad 2009, 225).

China has intervened heavily in currency markets to prevent the yuan/remninbi from appreciating. As a result, China's central bank must make large purchases of U.S. financial securities in order to support its currency (Morrison and Labonte 2, Setser 2). Rather than hold reserves in dollars, which accumulate no interest, the Chinese government has converted some of its foreign exchange holdings into financial securities (Morrison and Labonte 6). China faces the dilemma of being unable to maintain its current trade surplus while allowing its currency to appreciate against the dollar (Drezner 2010, 2). Setser and Pandey write, "From 2000 to the middle of 2008 China had to buy an ever-increasing quantity of foreign assets to keep its currency from rising, and consequently the scale of financing that China's government provided to the United States — properly measured — almost continuously increased" (23). This places China in the position of having to accumulate more and more reserves, which it can either invest or hold as reserves. The only alternative to accumulating reserves would be to allow their currency to appreciate, which China has thus far proved reluctant to do as result of their economic dependence on exports. This demonstrates that China is made vulnerable by holding this debt and how its holdings fit into China's broader economic goals.

Several options exist for pressuring debtor countries. The most dramatic option would be for China to dump securities, or threaten to dump securities, in response to U.S. policy. Such actions could have serious negative impacts on the American economy, and likely the global economy as a whole. Morrison and Labonte note, "Some economists contend that attempts by China to unload a large share of its U.S. securities holdings could have a significant negative impact on the U.S. economy (at least in the short run)" (2). However, large off-loadings would hurt the U.S. economy and demand for Chinese produced consumer goods, as well as put increased upward pressure on China's currency. A massive sell-off would likely go against China's economic interests and would diminish the value of Chinese held dollar-denominated securities resulting in a large loss on the sale (Morrison and Labonte 14).

There is also the possibility that smaller reductions would have a limited impact. Morrison and Labonte write, "The magnitude of the effect would depend on how many U.S. securities China sold; modest reductions would have negligible effects on the economy given the vastness of U.S. financial markets. For example, Japan gradually reduced its treasury holdings from $699.4 billion to $582.2 billion from August 2004 to September 2007, a decline of $117.2 billion. This shift appears to have had little noticeable impact on the U.S. economy." (12) The effect would depend on whether a reduction was gradual or sudden, and whether such a reduction was a part of influence attempts or just a change in investment goals — some suggest that China may seek to diversify asset holdings. A slow decline in the trade deficit and dollar would not be bad for the economy (Morrison and Labonte 13). This would cause the Chinese currency to appreciate and would likely have a leveling effect on the Sino-American trading relationship.

Creditors also have several more discrete options beyond large scale dumping of assets on the open market. Drezner writes, "These options include slowing down the purchase of new debt, refraining from such purchases altogether, shifting the composition of foreign holdings or talking down the debtor's currency" (12–15). Implicit threats have a coercive effect too and influence attempts that end at the threat stage are much more likely to be effective (Drezner 2009, 15 and Drezner 2003, 645).

China's holdings, despite being numerically large, reflect interdependence in the Sino-American relationship. Both China and the U.S. are dependent on one another in this relationship. The U.S. because China is by far the largest holder of U.S. debt and securities as well as major source of imported goods and China is dependent on the U.S. for a market for exports. Moreover, China must keep accumulating U.S. reserves, which in turn are often converted into securities, or alter its monetary policy something China has shown reluctance to do. China's long-term economic goals depend on a good relationship with the U.S. and stable access to markets for exports.

It is unlikely that China would dump U.S. securities on the open market as serious economic harms would result beyond any potential gains and the value of future repayment would also be greatly harmed. This reflects the difficulty of manipulating another state in a highly interdependent relationship as well as the potential limitations resulting from why China has acquired so much U.S. debt and securities.

China has the option of threatening to refuse to buy new debt or slowing the purchase of new debt. These options are far more likely to be used and would carry fewer risks and costs for China. However, China's ability to carry through with these threats is limited by current monetary policy. Actions that remain at the threat level are far more likely to be effective at achieving intended foreign policy gains than ones that actually have to be carried out (Drezner 2009, 9).

Stunning imbalances

This section examines some of the broader economic conditions that created China's trade surplus and the United States' complimentary trade imbalance. Broader imbalances within the international economic system and the Sino-American bilateral trade relationship created the conditions for this, and as long as they exist China will need to purchase U.S. debt and the United States will be in need of credit. China's undervaluing of the yuan is a large part of creating the conditions for these imbalances.

Many tie China's creditor status and the United States' debtor status to broader imbalances within the international economic system and the Sino-US relationship. Drezner describes these as "Stunning imbalances," wherein China and the United States fall on either side of an extreme, sustaining each other in the process. Consumption as a share of American GDP averaged 67 percent from 1975 to 2000, while China was at a global low of 38 percent (Roach 2009, 4 and Drezner 2009, 12). In the United States the personal savings rate was negative, while in China it approached fifty percent of GDP (Drezner 12). Prasad argues, "The United States and China together epitomize the sources and dangers of global macroeconomic imbalances" (2009, 223). Americans do not save very much; instead they consume whereas the Chinese save a substantial share of their income. These savings are then lent out to Western consumer countries (Ferguson and Schularick 2007, 228). All of this lending depresses the key long-term interest rate (in the United States) (Morrison and Labonte 2).

The United States' debt is problematic because it is coupled with a rising current account deficit, driven by a fall in personal savings and a rise in consumption (mostly in the form of imports). The twin budget and trade deficits have left the United States dependent on foreign borrowing; to fund this, creditors have purchased dollars and dollar-denominated assets (Drezner 2009, 11–12, Milner 1993, 306-307).

China's high national saving rate and its tightly managed currency support the export of cheap goods and cheap financing to support those goods. The consequences of this policy are now going back on China and the Chinese economy. As China continues to maintain a current account surplus, it has little alternative to buying U.S. treasury bonds with the reserves it accumulates as a result of managing its exchange rate (Prasad 2009, 223).

At the same time, the U.S. is in need of willing buyers of bonds as it continues to finance its budget deficit (Prasad 224). A gradual decrease in Chinese holding would not have a negative impact on the U.S. economy and may in fact be beneficial as this would reduce the trade deficit and create greater balances in the international economy (Morrison and Labonte 2).

Large outflows in capital are also potentially detrimental to the Chinese economy. As capital flows out of China, and for the most part into the developed world, opportunities for using this capital in China are lost. Prasad attributes this to the weakness of the financial sector in capital-exporting countries, such as China. This results in a limited ability to absorb and intermediate capital, and redistribute it throughout the domestic economy. This can hurt long-term economic growth and productivity (Prasad 2007, 187, 189).

The global imbalances that make this possible result from developed countries sustaining large current account deficits, (the United States among them), and developing countries maintaining large current account surpluses. Exporting capital to sustain these imbalances are often referred to as global imbalances. While these imbalances seem not to have triggered any kind of economic adjustments, they may have broader consequences for welfare. There may also be consequences resulting from the policies needed to sustain these imbalances (Prasad 2007, 190).

Prasad argues that China's currency policy results in a loss of ability to target monetary policy at domestic objectives through market instruments like interest rates (Prasad 191). A move towards increased reliance on domestic consumption — which comprises a small part of economic growth, which is heavily reliant on exports — would generate greater stability in the long run (Prasad 2009, 1).

China's national saving rate of 43 percent of GDP in 2003 is unusually high for any country (Blanchard and Giavazzi 2006, 3). Blanchard and Giavazzi advocate a decrease in Chinese savings rates, a corresponding increase in services, and an appreciation of the RMB (2). High savings and export-led growth do not have to accompany a large trade surplus — in order for this to be avoided investment should equal savings. (Blanchard and Giavazzi 8).

China's holdings of U.S. debt are tied to broader imbalances in the global economy. In the long run, it would not be bad for the Chinese or American economies if adjustments were to take place and current account imbalances were reduced. China's currency policy is responsible for the extremely high saving rate and China's large holdings of U.S. debt and reserves.

This results in interdependence between China and the U.S. as they make up corresponding sides of the broader global imbalances. As long as the policies that have created and sustained this imbalance are maintained, China and the U.S. will become locked in a debtor-creditor relationship, confined to the dependencies and risks that go along with it.

International monetary power

This section will provide an overview of the literature on economic and financial statecraft. This focuses on hard power relating to financial relations and applies to the potential power of a creditor over a debtor. Much of the literature focuses on the question of sanctions and coercion relating to adjustments in trade imbalances. While not directly related to the issue at hand, general concepts from these discussions can be applied to and used for the question of the power of creditors. There are several discussions specifically of the power of creditors in the literature, which will be discussed.

Andrews defines international monetary power as "when one state's behavior changes because of its monetary relationship with another state" and monetary statecraft as "the conscious manipulation of monetary relations in order to influence the policies of other states" (2006, 1). Drezner defines economic coercion as "the threat or act by a sender government or governments to disrupt economic exchange with a target state, unless the target acquiesces to a particular demand" (2003, 643). Both of these definitions cover the broad context of using financial power as a hard power asset. This hinges on a certain monetary relationship existing between actors and the conscious decision to use this to attempt to coerce the other actor.

For the most part, monetary statecraft is easier said than done. There are substantial impediments to the use of monetary power as a deliberate instrument of economic statecraft (Andrews 25). Andrews observes that, for the most part, financial power corresponds to influence rather than the ability to coerce or control (16). Influence is the capacity to have an effect on outcomes; however, influence is not the same as total control over outcomes that often accompanies successful coercion attempts but rather the ability to move policy outcomes in a favorable direction and have a say in decision making where one otherwise would not.

Moments when monetary pressure has been decisive are rare (Andrews 28). The financial and economic statecraft literature recognizes the limitations of financial power as a tool. It is often too unfocused and indiscriminate to be an effective tool (Andrews 27). Andrews writes, "The tools of monetary statecraft — especially those tools having to do with currency relations — are often too blunt to be effective when they would be desired and too diffuse to be directed at particular targets without incurring substantial collateral damage" (25). As a result, other hard power assets are often more useful.

The potential power given to a creditor is predicated by the need for new loans on the part of the debtor state and the potential to refuse such loans. Milner writes, "The debtor's weakness derives from the need for new loans. The creditor's strength flows from the ability to threaten to cut off new loans to the debtor or to curtail them if the debtor does not meet certain new conditions. Power for the creditor arises from the manipulation of the debtor's dependence in this bilateral relationship" (1993, 534). A few factors contribute to the extent of dependence and the potential for coercion. The first is the extent to which the debtor needs new loans, and what the cost of going without them would be. If the need is only minimal then the ability to impose costs on the debtor is limited. If the need is great then potential costs are much higher (Milner 1993, 534).

Second is the availability of alternative sources of credit (Milner 1993, 534). In order for a creditor to gain significant power, the debtor state must be unable to access alternative sources of credit (Drezner 2009, 18). Milner writes, "When credit is scarce or would come from elsewhere at a higher interest rate, creditors have the political leverage to make threats, and when creditors are states, providing credit can be an effective instrument of hard power" (316). If no alternative credit is available, then a creditor can become quite powerful. This is why institutions like the IMF and World Bank, which serve as lenders of last resort, have historically been so powerful and able to impose structural adjustment programs on debtors — although they have lost power in recent years with the emergence of creditors like China that are willing to give unconditional loans (Drezner 2009, 18). If other sources of credit are available, then the impact is marginal.

The third factor is that there must be low costs of retaliation. Great powers are rarely able to asymmetrically punish other great powers — their targets either possess no vulnerabilities, or have mutual vulnerabilities. This is why the success rate has been so low when two great powers have been involved (Drezner 2008, 19).

Drezner contends that, in the case of the United States and China, none of these criteria are met (20). The United States has alternative sources of credit, both domestic and foreign, and the United States would impose significant costs to China — especially if it went with the nuclear option of dumping debt on the open market.

When attempts are made by a creditor to manipulate a debtor, they often carry the potential of damaging the debtor economy, the creditor economy and the world economy as a whole. Chaos in the American economy would likely induce chaos globally (Milner 1993, 536-7). Another important deterrent is when debt is denominated in the debtor currency — as is the case with the United States and China — creditors do not want to devalue outstanding debt payment (Milner 555 and Drezner 2009, 20). Most of China's debt is denominated in USD, which leaves them vulnerable to exchange rate depreciation (Chin and Helleiner 2008, 94).

Another constraint is concerns over general relations between the creditor and debtor country. If the two are extensively involved in other areas, manipulating the debt is difficult since they are intertwined in the other's relations. Milner writes, "The special place of the United States in the international system means that its international relations with other states are likely to involve complex webs of financial, commercial, military and political ties" (537). The importance of the U.S. market to China highlights the state of mutual dependence they are in (Drezner 2009, 21).

Globalization changes the nature of monetary power and monetary diplomacy; however, it does not eliminate it all together. Kirshner writes, "it does not provide an escape from politics; even under globalization international relations will continue to feature currency manipulation, monetary dependence and strategic disruption" (Kirshner 2006, 161). Globalization does not eliminate the potential for competition, influence and coercion; however, it changes the environment and manner in which it takes place.

Power exists in the case of asymmetric dependence, where one actor is more dependent on a relationship than the other (Cooper 2006, 164). Keohane and Nye write, "When we say that asymmetrical interdependence can be a source of power we are thinking of power as control over resources or the potential to affect outcomes. A less dependent actor in a relationship often has a significant political resource because changes in the relationship (which the actor may be able to initiate or threaten) will be less costly to that actor than to its partners" (11). In the case of debtor-creditor status this can mean that if one actor is more dependent on this relationship then the other may be able to manipulate it. Economic relations often involve linkages and mutual dependencies, however these relations are often asymmetrical. Opportunities may exist for the actor that is less dependent or has greater autonomy in the relationship (Cohen 2008, 33).

In terms of the Sino-American debtor-creditor relationship, the question of symmetry is important. If China has a need to issue credit and acquire assets that are mirrored by American needs for purchases of additional debt, then neither party has power over the other. There are several reasons why symmetry is present. For different reasons, both actors seek stability in the relationship: China, because they seek repayment on previously issued debt, and the United States, because they wish to see continued Chinese purchases of debt. As a result of China's currency policy they have little choice but to continue to acquire assets — a decision that would likely result in currency appreciation otherwise. This cancels out any upper hand China may have otherwise gained. As a result, costs of any coercion attempts are likely higher than the intended benefits in policy concessions.

None of the three criteria-- need for new loans (and costs of going without), alternative source of credit and low costs of retaliation-- are present in the case of the United States and China. American access to alternative sources of credit — albeit at potentially higher interest rates depending on the levels of Chinese threats or refusal to buy new debt — limits the power of a creditor to impose significant costs. Mutual dependence between the United States and China, and linkages resulting from overall relations limits China's ability to insulate itself from retaliation and negative impacts on the American economy.

Another factor not discussed in the above literature is China's reasons for purchasing and amassing U.S. debt and reserves, which is their currency policy. So long as China seeks to maintain currency stability they have little alternative to continued purchases and accumulation of U.S. assets.

While there are serious limits on the utility of monetary statecraft, the literature reflects broader trends towards globalization and interdependence that influence Sino-American relations. So far, this paper has established that the debtor-creditor relationship between China and the U.S. results from broader economic trends and ties. China's status as an exporter and the U.S' need for imports of cheap goods creates ties between them that would result in mutual harms should one of them target the other. China must consider their general relationship with the U.S. and its value to their broader development goals in deciding whether threats or use of monetary statecraft would be useful for achieving policy goals.

Theoretical perspectives

This section will examine the perceived role of China and supposed level of threat to the United States in realist and liberal international relations theories. Realism dominates general discussions of Sino-U.S. relations and has framed perceptions of this issue in specific (Guo and Teng, Pant, Zhao and Meideros). Liberalism is used because it takes into account complex interdependence and provides substantial explanatory power for Sino-U.S. relations in general and this issue in specific (Meideros and Ali).

These theories will be employed to help explain my more hands-on observations and provide a general framework for viewing Sino-U.S. relations. It is important to account for overall Sino-U.S. relations when discussing the power China may exert as a creditor and whether conflict between China and the United States is likely or beneficial.

Realism frames the Sino-American relationship within the context of great power politics and conflict. China is seen as an emerging power that has the potential to challenge the U.S. While the U.S. is seen as the sole superpower and despite showing some signs of decline will defend its position and attempt to maintain supremacy (Zhao 2008, 4–5). If this is the case then China will try to gain power over the U.S. and if possible use any sources of influence to achieve policy gains. This frames the Sino-American relationship as conflicting and reflects the general assumptions of much of the rhetoric on this issue.

Liberalism focuses on how complex interdependence between China and the U.S. limits the potential for conflict and creates the potential for non-zero sum outcomes (Subacchi 2008, 5 and Zhao 2008, 8–9). Within this context, interdependence, particularly economic interdependence, is a key element. Both states are locked in the relationship for different reasons and are mutually dependent on the relationship. This limits the potential for conflict, although there is still the potential for competition.

By comparing the two theoretical frameworks we can better evaluate the Sino-American relationship and the influence of complex interdependence. Mutual interdependence is a significant factor in the debtor-creditor relationship and must be properly accounted for. The likelihood of conflict is a significant factor in whether the potential risks associated with dumping securities, reducing the number of securities purchased or the threat thereof would be perceived as tolerable by China. If conflict is more pervasive than cooperation, the stability of the Sino-American relationship will be less valued, and power and policy gains will be more important. If cooperation and economic interdependence are more important then the risks will likely be perceived as prohibitive.

Complex interdependence

Complex interdependence theory, as presented by Robert Keohane and Joseph Nye in Power and Interdependence, argues that as transnational connections (interdependencies) between states and societies decreases the use of force and the occurrence of power balancing. As a result of increased linkages all countries are sensitive and vulnerable to other countries (Guo and Teng 3). The reduction of military force and increase in economic and other forms of interdependence should increase the probability of peaceful cooperation among states (Guo and Teng 4). Keohane and Nye argue that balance of power theories and national security imagery are poorly adapted to analyzing problems of economic interdependence (1989, 8).

China places a strong emphasis on internal priorities, including development, improving quality of life and social stability — social stability is strongly tied to development and economic growth, and is often termed GNPism. The Chinese Communist Party (CCP) draws legitimacy from continued economic growth. China needs a peaceful international environment and strong ties with the United States to sustain continued economic growth. China's success during the reform era has resulted from embracing globalization and economic integration with the global market (Guo and Teng 4). China has no reason to take actions that would threaten economic stability and access to markets.

While China may want to play a larger role in international economic institutions — as is natural for an emerging great power — they benefit greatly from integration into the global economy and are effectively a status quo power. In terms of Sino-American relations, one of China's top priorities is ensuring access to American markets (Meideros 15–16 and Drezner 33). Confrontation and conflict with the Americans would achieve the opposite result.

Power

While power is an essentially contested concept there are many different definitions present in the international relations literature (Barnett and Duvall 40–41 and Newmann). There is more agreement in the economic and financial state-craft literature because conceptions of power exist within the context of specific circumstances of financial power. For the purposes of this paper, power will be defined as "the ability in various forms of one agent to impose its will on another in doing so, it concentrates on power relations between states and the interaction between their ability to impose economic outcomes, military and geo-political power and the structural power of some states to shape the terms of the international economy" (Milner 1993, 310). This definition is state-centric, focusing on the relations between states and downplaying the effect of other actors. Power is a relative concept and not everyone can have equal power — however in the case of great powers high degrees of power are typically present (Subacchi 2008, 1).

This definition is selected because it applies to the context of the U.S. and China. It deals with the interactions of states, while ignoring other actors, which is fitting for the case under study. It works within a liberal-realistic framework while ignoring the considerations of feminist, Marxist and social constructivist thinkers for three reasons. First, because liberalism and realism Sare the two theories that provide the most explanatory value for this issue. Second, because this definition is suited to analyzing the interactions of two major powers. And third, one actor's ability to impose its will on another is at the heart of financial power.

Power can be divided into external (influence) and internal dimensions (autonomy) — the distinction between the two is significant (Cohen 32). While they are interrelated, they are not of equal importance (Cohen 6). Autonomy addresses policy independence or the ability "to exercise policy independence, act freely, insulated from outside pressure in policy formulation and implementation. In this sense, power does not mean influencing others, it means not allowing others to influence you" (Cohen 2008, 32). In this sense, an actor is powerful because they are able to act freely and is insulated from outside pressure. Once an actor can sustain a high degree of autonomy, then they can exercise authority elsewhere (Cohen 2008, 6). Cohen observes, "First and foremost, policy makers must be free (or at least relatively free) to pursue national objectives in the specific issue area or relationship without outside constraint, to avoid compromise or sacrifices to accommodate the interests of others" (33) The second element is influence, "the ability to shape events or outcomes." This consists of control over the behavior of other actors and often takes the form of coercion. It is possible to have autonomy without influence but autonomy is required for influence (Andrews 2006, 33). Ideally, a state would like to influence other states without being influenced in the process.

It is one thing to claim that power resources exist and another to manipulate them in order to pursue specific outcomes. Andrews notes, "Such undertakings — or influence attempts — are purposeful acts; they are means toward an end, intended to bring about desired changes in the behavior of others" (17). Just because one has power does not mean that one is going to use it.

Potential constraints on Chinese use of financial power include their monetary policy, and broader economic dependence on the U.S, as well as their need for repayment on existing debt and assets. If China were to harm the U.S. economy, they would see a huge loss on these assets and on exports generally. This dependence gives the U.S. a greater ability to resist Chinese pressure and acts as a limit on China's ability to coerce the U.S.

It is often difficult to use perceived power resources to achieve specific goals (Cohen 2006, 6). The American perception that China has power as a result of its holdings could itself be a potential source of power (Friedman 1998,75–76 and Drezner 2009, 8). However, it is often far more difficult to achieve actual gains from this perceived power. Some power resources don't translate to or are lost in producing outcomes through political bargaining (Keohane and Nye 1989, 11). This is important to consider in analyzing the potential transfer of financial power to other areas.

Realists perceive power in terms of power balancing and zero sum outcomes (Guo and Teng 3). Power is to be used to help achieve policy goals, which often come at the expense of other actors. If an actor like China is on the rise that means that other actors will have less power. In these terms states seek to keep and gain power, and only cooperate when it is in their self-interest to do so (Pant 2011, 2–4).

By contrast, liberals view power as being used in subtler and more cooperative ways. Power does not always come at the expense of another actor and cooperation can often be beneficial. Since mutual dependencies make conflict extremely harmful, other forms of influence attempts and competition are emphasized (Subacchi 2008, 5, Clegg 2009,14–15 and Meideros 15–16).

Realism

There are two predominant views of China. The first is that of realists (often referred to as China pessimists) (Pant, Zhao and Guo and Teng). This view conceives of Sino-American relations as the product of great power politics and China as a rising power that is challenging and will threaten the United States. Guo and Teng write, "According to Hans Morgenthau, a new rising power will naturally want to challenge the status quo, thus making it less peaceful unless there is some sort of balance of power to tame the new power." This line of thought contends that the rise of a new power has never been peaceful and a power struggle is inevitable (3). Relations will be zero-sum as opposed to cooperative. Despite growing economic ties and globalization realists argue that conflict for supremacy will occur. Pant rejects the idea of interdependence creating peace and "as China emerges as a global power, it will expand its military footprint across the globe, like other great powers throughout history" (Pant 2011, 2). Hegemonic states, such as the United States, have a vested interest in maintaining the current international system "because their values and interests are often universalized to the point where they largely conform to the rules, values, and institutions of the system. Rising powers, however, often demand a change in the power hierarchy and become challengers to the established system." Historically, power competition has often resulted in conflicts and sometimes large-scale wars. China is not currently at parity with the U.S. but it is a rising power (Zhao 2008, 4). The U.S. will fight to ensure continued primacy and this could be a source of conflict between the U.S. and China (Pant 2011, 3).

Chinese authoritarianism is worrying to many Americans (Zhao 2008, 7). There are concerns that China will replace the Washington consensus built around free markets and liberal democracy with the Beijing consensus based on authoritarian government, rapid economic growth and stability. Zhao writes,

> The rise of popular nationalist sentiments and China's reluctance to open domestic political competition to build a liberal democracy, has exacerbated the sense of unease among many Americans about an increasingly powerful China. Many have concerns about China's aspirations for great power status drawing upon strong nationalism linked with the victim's conviction of a ‚century of shame and humiliation' at the hands of imperialist powers. (2008, 7)

China is viewed as potentially threatening the American way of life and system of values. This is fitting with Samuel Huntington's idea of the clash of civilizations and democratic peace theory. This casts the West (U.S.) as one civilization or unique cultural entity, which will clash with China, another major civilization (Huntington 1993). Democratic peace theory argues that authoritarian governments are far more likely to go to war than democracies, which rarely if ever fight one another. Because China is an authoritarian state it is threatening to America's ideals and way of life, and is more likely to go to war with the U.S. (Zhao 2008, 7).

Liberalism

The other major school of though on Sino-American relations is the liberals (often referred to as China optimists) (Meideros, Subacchi and Clegg). Liberals argue that China's rise will be peaceful and will not result in threat-based bipolarity (Jia 2008, 45). China may be rising but it can and should be integrated into the international system and conflict can be prevented. Ali argues, "China's growing stature and comprehensive national power would guarantee it could not be taken for granted, but there was no evidence that it posed a direct or immediate challenge to either America or the U.S.-led order" (2012, 18). China's growth is part of the growth of Asia and the developing world and migration of industry based on comparative advantage lines (Roach 2009, 3–4).

Both countries should recognize their semi-symbiotic linkages. The best strategy is cooperation, which will ensure that both are strong powers (Jia 53). China's socio-economic goals give them no reason to challenge the status quo. Beijing sees preservation of domestic stability — the threat of disruption by pro-democracy movements and challenges to leadership — as one of its most important internal security challenges. China has a diplomatic focus on ensuring access to commodities, energy supplies, and markets.

This means that China is likely to prioritize mutual benefits that can be had from stable economic and diplomatic relations with the U.S. and is unlikely to threaten these. Whatever policy concessions could be gained as a result of threatening to dump assets or actually selling them off would be marginal compared to the harms that would result. China is moving beyond their territorial interests and becoming a global actor. This is mostly benign. They are contributing troops to peacekeeping missions, as demonstrated by Chinese contributions to the international anti-piracy force in in the Gulf of Aden and Indian Ocean (Ali 2012, 18). Chinese participation can be taken one of two ways: either as a worrying expansion of Chinese power projection or as a sign of China's willingness to join America and the international community in collaborative and collective security missions.

Guo and Teng argue that integration enhances cooperation and interdependence. China's vulnerability creates a common bond with the rest of the world (4–6). Zhao writes, "Liberal optimists believe that globalization has produced growing strategic interdependence among great powers. This strategic interdependence constrains the USA and China from pursuing zero-sum strategies towards each other" (2008, 4). Beijing's leaders have taken a pragmatic position to maintain a cooperative relationship because they realize that China's continuing economic rise rests on the maintenance of a favorable international environment, the most important element of which is a cooperative relationship with the USA (Zhao 2008, 9). Zhao observes that this was behind the concept of "China's peaceful rise" in 2003 at the Bao Forum (an annual gathering of high-level business and political leaders from the Asia-Pacific) and what President Hu Jintao later referred to as "peaceful development" at the 2004 Bao Forum (2008, 23).

Comparison and applications

By seeing China as a threatening power, there is the risk of creating a self-fulfilling prophecy in which China responds to perceived antagonisms in kind. Realists fail to account for the high levels of interdependence between China and the United States.

The United States has played a large part in drawing China into the international community and creating strong linkages. If the United States can accommodate increased Chinese interests and power then their rise is likely to be peaceful and both will benefit. If the United States views China as a threat then they will sabotage potential opportunities to take advantage of linkages.

If the United States were to become entangled in a serious conflict with China, this would disrupt trade flows — leaving the United States scrambling to adjust to the absence of easy flows of cheap consumer goods — and would limit capital flows — on which the United States is heavily dependent due to continued budget deficits.

China's economy would be seriously harmed by high-level conflict. The United States accounts for a significant amount of trade with China. Some argue that China has other serious trading partners but disrupting that amount of trade flows would have serious negative repercussions for the Chinese economy and subsequently the CCP's claims on legitimacy.

It is difficult to imagine an issue where China and the United States would have such divergent opinions that the benefits of conflict would significantly outweigh the negative economic and political consequences of such. This is not to say that the United States and China will agree on all issues but linkages do limit the means available for attempted coercion and influence attempts.

Another limitation is that hard power resources that can be employed successfully against middle and lesser powers are often of limited use against other great powers. They will either have a limited ability to impose costs on the other actor or will incur significant costs themselves through influence attempts. In some cases dependencies and vulnerabilities may be asymmetric and it is in these situations that influence attempts are likely to be far more successful. On many issues, China and the United States will either cooperate or decide to agree to disagree — as is the current policy on Taiwan (Ali 2008, 18).

Increased cooperation and interdependence does not preclude differences of opinion on certain issues (Zhao 2008, 4). Keohane and Nye suggest that conflict will not disappear but will take new forms (1989, 8). As an emerging power, China has taken advantage of rising power and has defended its interests by both cooperative and coercive means. China cooperates on areas of mutual interest and "it has also used its strategic assets to thwart U.S. objectives, including using or threatening to use force, forming alliances to curb U.S. power and voting against proposals favorable to the USA in international organizations" (Zhao 2008, 9).

The Sino-American relationship is extremely complicated. Zhao observes, "The USA and China in recent decades have cooperated more and more often on many fronts but have also found themselves in sharp disagreement on many contentious issues" (10). These include Taiwan, China's military modernization, U.S. unilateralism, energy security, trade imbalance and the D.P.R.K. It is in these areas that China is less willing to cooperate with the United States (Pant 2011, 15).

These sticky issues are important for understanding the overall Sino-U.S. relationship. Saunders argues that China poses the most difficult strategic challenge to the USA — being marked by both cooperative and competitive elements (119). Meideros writes, "China's diversification strategy is altering the conduct of U.S.-China relations. As the sources of China's prosperity, security and status have broadened (and during a period in which China perceives that the United States is in relative decline), Beijing is becoming less willing to accommodate U.S. preferences and more able to resist pressure from Washington" (xxiii). As China grows in power, it will be more willing to resist American pressure and issues and to assert itself. However, China will also strive to maintain good relations with the U.S. and other advanced industrialized states because of the economic benefits of doing so. Both cooperation and competition are likely to occur depending on the situation. Conflict between the U.S. and China is highly unlikely due to the high costs that would result from mutual interdependence.

Chinese Strategic Influence During the Financial Crisis

In this section, attempts by the Chinese to use financial power during the financial crisis will be examined. This serves as a good case study for whether or not China has been able to convert financial power into political power and concessions from the United States as it was a time period in which China had large holdings of American debt, as well as when the United States was in the position of needing new loans — as a result of the bailout out and the U.S. government stimulus package. It will also serve as a means of testing the applicability of realism and liberalism in the context of the Sino-American debtor-creditor relationship.

China's status as a capital exporter has increased its influence in international financial institutions and with smaller states. From 2006 onwards, China has been able to prevent the IMF from investigating their currency — in large part due to their strong financial situation. China has used its influence to veto Asian Development Bank loans to India due to a territorial dispute. In 2007, China's State Administration of Foreign Exchange (SAFE) purchased $300 million in Costa Rican bonds in exchange for Costa Rica switching recognition to Beijing from Taiwan (Drezner 2010, 2). China sees credit as a means of reducing Taiwan's international space. China has used its creditor status to gain access to resources securing $40 billion in oil deals with Russian, Iranian, Venezuelan and Brazilian firms. China has more power over these countries because they have a harder time getting capital (Drezner 2).

This increased influence which has been used to exact preferred policies and access to resources, was used with weaker states and the same conditions are unlikely to be present when dealing with a state like the U.S. These states have limited access to credit, which is not true of the U.S. Furthermore, they do not have the same kind of interdependent economic relationship with China that the U.S. does.

China's influence over the U.S. is far more limited. During this time China was able to exact minimal concessions from the United States — and only in concert with other creditors — despite high levels of rhetoric. China has been able to use its creditor status to coerce lesser states that have a harder time getting credit and has been able to gain significant autonomy (Drezner 2009, 32 and Dyer 2012). It has used this autonomy to resist and decrease American pressure on sensitive issues. Drezner writes, "To date China has translated its large capital surplus into minimal foreign policy gains [with the United States]" (10). During the credit crunch of 2008–2009, the United States became increasingly dependent on Chinese credit. As the crisis worsened, China became increasingly outspoken about their desire for reform of the international monetary system. Drezner argues that this time period can serve as a test case for whether China's has been able to convert financial power into political power (31).

China had two primary policy demands on the U.S. The first was that China wanted guaranteed access to American markets. Despite World Trade Organization membership by both China and the U.S., the U.S. faced domestic pressure to engage in protectionist measures including anti-dumping measures, health and safety regulations and was calling China a currency manipulator (Roach 2009, 6). Between 2005 and 2007, Congress introduced 45 anti-China trade bills although none of them passed (Drezner 2009,33). This reflects a desire on the part of the Chinese to maintain stable access to American markets, which is in keeping with liberal theories. China sought to guarantee what they see as an essential element of economic success.

The second was protection of Chinese assets (guarantees of repayment). By the summer of 2008, China had moved to riskier U.S. assets like high-yield bonds and equities and, by June 2008, more than half of their holdings were outside treasury bonds (Drezner 2009, 32). This reflects an attempt on China's part to avoid the risks associated with their investments. By moving into higher risk investments and due to losses resulting financial crisis (particularly holdings in Fannie Mae and Freddie) China was exposed to potential significant loses (Drezner 32 and Dyer 2012).

During the fall of 2008, China persistently pressured the United States but failed to receive policy concessions on asset (bonds and equities) protection (Drezner 33). In response in August 2008, Chinese financial institutions stopped buying new assets and started selling off existing assets due to concerns that the United States government would let Fannie Mae and Freddy Mac collapse. A month later, the bailout was passed, and Fannie Mae and Freddy Mac were put under conservatorship, moving partially — but not all the way — towards meeting China's demands.

International pressure played a large role in this decision — this came from China as well as Russia, Saudi Arabia and other major creditors. There were concerns that foreign creditors would start dumping American investments. Domestic pressure and the collapse of the American housing market also played a role (Drezner 2009, 34–35).

This demonstrates both Chinese strength and vulnerability. China was seeking to protect future repayment and to avoid losses as a result of their holdings. It also shows that the U.S. was willing to consider the demands of its creditors in making domestic policy decisions. However, China only had a marginal influence on the decision. Domestic pressures and other international creditors also played a role. China would not have been able to achieve their goals independently.

Throughout the fall of 2008, the United States officially requested continued Chinese purchases of dollars, to which Chinese officials demanded government guarantees of debt. American officials refused such a guarantee. China showed displeasure by being a net seller of U.S. debt in November 2008 — the first time China was a net seller in two years (Drezner 36). Setser describes as the "first concrete demonstration of China's financial leverage" (21). China's actions intentionally imposed costs on the United States. However, this had no affect on U.S. policy. Despite the selloffs, neither Bush nor Obama made concessions on the guarantees. The economic effect was only temporary with the assets recovering in 2009 (Drezner 36–37).

Chinese officials continued to make statements saying they would abstain from future purchases if the U.S. did not change their policy. They failed to receive guarantees of access to American markets and the government of the United States did not protect other Chinese assets as requested — Morgan Stanley and Blackstone plummeted causing massive loses and public backlash in China (Drezner 37).

A refusal to move on guarantees was likely due to the fact that the costs of guarantees, both politically and financially, would be much greater than any costs that refusal to buy new debt and dumping of assets would impose. In the case of the decision to bailout key American financial institutions both domestic and international pressures played a role — creditors had more power because they acted in concert, as opposed to China acting alone in requesting guarantees. The pressures to place these institutions under protection were much higher and the political costs of the decision were much lower. If China is to have success in pressuring the United States using its creditor status, the costs of their demands must be lower than the costs they are able to impose through coercion.

With the prospect of $2 trillion in new U.S. debt to be issued in 2009, Chinese officials and Chinese think tanks compiled wish lists and Chinese officials increased rhetoric (Drezner 2009, 38). The Chinese Prime Minister voiced concerns over the direction of U.S. fiscal policy and challenged the use of the dollar as reserve currency. Drezner writes, "China's threats and rhetoric failed to yield significant policy concessions" (38). The United States dropped talk of Chinese currency manipulation but protectionism continued as did a refusal to guarantee debt. Drezner attributes failures to Chinese dependence on U.S. markets (Drezner 40). China's only success in attempted coercion was on Fannie Mae and Freddy Mac, where it acted in concert with other sovereign creditors — including Russia, Japan and Saudi Arabia.

Overall these interactions do not demonstrate aggression or conflict on the part of China but rather attempts to mitigate potential losses on investments and to ensure access to markets. The later fits with China's long term economic and development goals. Stability in the Sino-U.S. relationship is privileged. The former reflects China's desire for repayment, a source of vulnerability.

China has been more aggressive with lesser powers to which it is a creditor. These relationships are marked by asymmetric dependencies on which China is less dependent. However, the same conditions are not present with the U.S. Mutual dependencies exist that prevent any real policy gains from being achieved by either China or the U.S. Chinese officials did not carry through on their threats to abstain from future purchases, in large part because they need to continue purchases to maintain their monetary policy.

China has been able to use its creditor status to gain significant levels of autonomy, including having the United States back off on human rights issues and on accusations of currency manipulation. China was able to ignore U.S. pressure and allowed the yuan to depreciate during the financial crisis and during Hillary

Clinton's February 2009 trip to Beijing when she stated that human rights concerns would take a back seat to economic issues (Kessler 2009). China could not compel the U.S. to achieve significant policy concessions on asset protection or protectionism but was also able to resist pressure (Drezner 2009, 42).

Creditors are commonly regarded as gaining in autonomy as a result of being free from potential pressure from creditors as a result of the influence they gain from potentially acting as a creditor to others. While it may not significantly contribute to coercion capabilities, financial power can significantly bolster autonomy. In terms of the Sino-U.S. relationship, this is significant in areas of disagreement such as human rights, currency manipulation and Taiwan. China will be more able to resist influence attempts from the United States, and has shown as much so far.

The typical conception that creditors are strong and debtors are weak does not hold true except in the case of autonomy. China does gain in autonomy and has been able to resist American pressure, whereas China has been able to achieve a small amount of influence on some American policies. Autonomy gives China the ability to resist the U.S. while providing the grounds to apply pressure to the U.S., albeit often unsuccessfully. There are no signs that China views its holdings of U.S. debt securities as a hard power asset that could potentially be used in conflict with the U.S. The likelihood of conflict is limited, however competition is still occurring as liberalism and complex interdependence suggest.

As China grows in power and gains in autonomy they will be more able to resist American pressure on sensitive issues. On balance China's ability to influence the U.S. as a result of their creditor status is limited. This is due in large part to a lack of asymetrical dependencies in the Sino-American debtor-creditor relationship. This comes from the mutual dependence that is the broader Sino-American relationship. China is reliant on the U.S. as an export market, while the U.S. is reliant on China for cheap imports. Their debtor-creditor relationship is another side of this mutual dependence. It creates linkages, dependencies and vulnerabilities on the part of both states.

Conclusion

This paper aimed to analyze whether Chinese financial power will be transferable to other types of power in great power politics with the United States. Rhetoric by various politicians has greatly exaggerated the potential utility of financial power in other realms. China has been unable to use its creditor status to coerce the United States and has thus far only been able to achieve minimal policy concessions, while acting in concert with other creditors. China has used its creditor status to make gains with lesser powers, especially those that have limited access to credit. However, this is not likely to be repeated with a super power such as the United States. Asymmetric dependencies are not present in the Sino-American debtor-creditor relationship — with each locked in the relationship for different reason — so the opportunity for advantage is absent. China is heavily dependent on the American economy as an export market. This complex interdependence between the United States and China makes it difficult for China to successfully impose costs on the United States without damaging its own economy in the process.

Broader global financial imbalances contribute to China's current account surplus and the United States current account deficit. In the long run it may be beneficial for China to allow its currency to appreciate and to increase domestic consumption thereby decreasing reliance on exports. Thus would eliminate the need for China to accumulate U.S. reserves and purchase U.S. assets. As it now stands China has little choice but to continue to buy U.S. assets to maintain currency stability.

China has gained significant autonomy as a result of its creditor status and has been able to get the United States to reduce pressure on several sensitive issues. In this way China's creditor status plays against the United States, as it will reduce the ability of the United States to pressure China on currency policy, human rights issues and Taiwan. China may not be able to use its financial power to coerce the United States, but it can use these assets to prevent the United States from coercing it.

Bibliography

Ali, S. Mahmud. "Prologue: Shifting Tectonic Plates." Ed. S. Mahmud Ali. Asia-Pacific Security Dynamics in the Obama Era: A New World Emerging. Abingdon, Oxon: Routledge, 2012. 1-18.

Ali, S. Mahmud. "Obama's Early Initiatives and Beijing's Response." Asia-Pacific Security Dynamics in the Obama Era: A New World Emerging. Abingdon, Oxon: Routledge, 2012. 19-58. At this point I would say that you have an over reliance on this author. You're going to have to look to balance it out a little better in order to show better research.

Andrews, David M. "Monetary Power and Monetary Statecraft." Ed. David M. Andrews. International Monetary Power. Ithaca, NY: Cornell UP, 2006. 7-30.

Barnett, Michael, and Raymond Duvall. "Power in International Politics." International Organization 59.1 (2005): 39-75.

Blanchard, Olivier, and Francesco Giavazzi. "Rebalancing Growth in China: A Three-handed Approach." China & World Economy 14.4 (2006): 1-20.

Chin, Gregory, and Eric Helleiner. "China as a Creditor: A Rising Financial Power?" Journal of International Affairs 62.1 (2008): 87-102.

Clegg, Jenny. China's Global Strategy: Towards a Multipolar World. London: Pluto, 2009.

Cohen, Benjamin J. "The Macrofoundations of Monetary Power." International Monetary Power. Ed. David M. Andrews. Ithaca, NY: Cornell UP, 2006. 31-50.

Cohen, Benjamin J. "The International Monetary System: DiffU.S.ion and Ambiguity." International Affairs (2008).

Cooper, Scott. "The Limits of Monetary Power: Statecraft within Currency Areas." International Monetary Power. Ed. David M. Andrews. London: Cornell UP, 2006. 162-83.

Drezner, Daniel W. "Bad Debts Assessing China's Financial Influence in Great Power Politics." International Security 34.2 (2009): 7-45.

Drezner, Daniel W. "The Hidden Hand of Economic Coercion." International Organization 57.3 (2003): 643-59.

Drezner, Daniel W. U.S. Debt to China: Implications and RepercU.S.sions. Proc. of U.S.-China Economic and Security Review Commission. 2010. 1-6.

Dyer, Geoff. "China's Dollar Dilemma." Financial Times. 2 Feb. 2009. Web. 22 Apr. 2012. <http://www.ft.com/cms/s/0/299e404c-011b-11de-8f6e-000077b07658.html#axzz1skTz9hQi>.

Ferguson, Niall, and Moritz Schularick. "'Chimerica' and the Global Asset Market Boom." International Finance 10.3 (2007): 215-39.

Friedman, Benjamin M. Day of Reckoning: The Consequences of American Economic Policy under Reagan and after. New York: Random House, 1988.

Huntington, Samuel P. "The Clash of Civilizations." Foreign Affairs 72.3 (1993): 22-49.

Jia, Qingguo. "Learning to Live with the Hegemon: China's Policy toward the U.S.A. since the End of the Cold War." China-US Relations Transformed. Ed. Suisheng Zhao. London: Routledge, 2008. 45-57.

Keohane, Robert O., and Joseph S. Nye. Power and Interdependence. Glenview, IL: Scott, Foresman, 1989

Kessler, Glenn. "Experts Divided Over Whether Clinton Should Push China on Human Rights." Washington Post. The Washington Post, 23 Feb. 2009. Web. 22 Apr. 2012. <http://www.washingtonpost.com/wp-dyn/content/article/2009/02/22/AR2009022200867.html>

Kirshner, Jonathan. "Currency and Coercion in the Twenty-First Century." International Monetary Power. Ed. David M. Andrews. London: Cornell UP, 2006. 139-61.

Milner, Helen. "American Debt and World Power." International Journal Ethnic Tension & Nationalism 48.3 (1993): 527-60.

Newmann, Saul. "The Place of Power in Political Discourse." International Political Science Review / Revue Internationale De Science Politique 25.2 (2004): 139-57.

Pant, Harsh V. China's Rising Global Profile: The Great Power Tradition. Brighton: SU.S.sex Academic, 2011.

Prasad, Eswar S. "Effects of the Financial Crisis on the U.S.-China Economic Relationship." Cato Journal 29.2 (2009): 223-35.

Prasad, Eswar. "The Welfare Implications of Global Financial Flows." Cato Journal 27.2 (2007): 185-92.

Prasad, Eswar. "Rebalancing Growth in Asia." Finance and Development (2009): 19-22.

Prasad, Eswar S. Rebalancing Growth in Asia. Working paper no. 15169. Cambridge, MA: National Bureau of Economic Research, 2009.

Roach, Stephen S. A Wake-up Call for the US and China: Stress Testing a Symbiotic Relationship. Rep. 2009.

Rogers, Simon. "US Debt: How Big Is It and Who Owns It?" The Guardian. Guardian News and Media, 03 Aug. 2011. Web. 21 Apr. 2012. <http://www.guardian.co.uk/news/datablog/2011/jul/15/us-debt-how-big-who-owns>.

Saunders, Phillip C. "Managing a Multifaceted Relationship between the U.S.A. and China." China-US Relations Transformed. Ed. Suisheng Zhao. London: Routledge, 2008. 119-40.

Setser, Brad. What to Do with over a Half a Trillion a Year? Understanding the Changes in the Management of China's Foreign Assets. Rep. Council of Foreign Relations, 2008.

Setser, Brad W., and Arpana Pandey. China's $1.5 Trillion Bet: Understanding China's External Portfolio. Working paper. Council of Foreign Relations.

Setser, Brad. "China: Creditor to the Rich." China Security 4.4 (2008): 17-23.

Subacchi, Paola. "New Power Centres and New Power Brokers: Are They Shaping a New Economic Order?" International Affairs 84.3 (2008): 485-98.

United States. Cong. China's Holdings of U.S. Securities: Implications for the U.S. Economy. By Wayne M. Morrison and Marc Labonte. 110 Cong., 1 sess. Cong. Rept. 2008.

Zhao, Suisheng. "Implications of China's Rise for U.S.-China Relations." China-US Relations Transformed. London: Routledge, 2008. 3-19.

Zhao, Suisheng. "China Rising: Geo-strategic Thrust and Diplomatic Engagement." China-US Relations Transformed. London: Routledge, 2008. 20-42.

Refugees on the World Stage

The troubling status of refugees in the Americas and in Africa and what can be done to improve their situation.

Mikias Tilahun Wondyfraw
Miami University, written while studying at the Global College of Long Island University in Costa Rica

Abstract

This independent research project analyzes the history and current landscape of international refugee law and it explores the treatment of refugees in four distinct contexts: two in the Americas and two in Africa. In the end, the author finds that while a considerable amount of international law calls for the humane treatment of refugees, the reality of the situation is much bleaker. Concluding that the United Nations is failing to uphold their own standards, the author offers solutions on what can be done to improve conditions for refugees the world over.

Introduction

> I urge you to celebrate the extraordinary courage and contribu-
> tions of refugees past and present.

> – United Nations Secretary General Kofi Annan

This independent research project focused on the foundation of international law
and its correlation with the Universal Declaration of Human Rights, the 1951
and the 1961 Conventions on Refugees and other regional conventions that form
the bases of today's international system. During my two weeks long research
project, I read philosophical, theoretical, and historical texts that were used to
write the Universal Declaration of Human Rights and the main tenants of international law. These texts, in additition to the research I conducted, allowed me to
determine whether international law can be applied as a tool to effectively combat
global injustice. The two weeks worth of field work consisted of traveling to the
University for Peace (UPEACE) in Ciudad Colon, Costa Rica. There, I took a sem-
inar on African Human Rights and interviewed students and faculty members
about their understanding of international law and refugees. My focus concerned
the Americas and Africa since these regions experienced imperialism and colo-
nialism by similar European countries.

My motivation to study international law is to understand if it is a western
concept or universal concept. In addition, I would like to know if international
law respects world diversity in all aspects of life. The core of my study will inquire,
if these are still a good basis to ensure justice or if there are other important components to take into consideration. For instance, my project will focus on two
case studies on 1) the African Institute for Human Rights and Development as
compared to the treatment of refugees in Guinea and 2) the treatment of refugees
in Salve as compared to the Haitian Centers Council for the Return of Haitian
Refugees. I want to know what it takes to defend the marginalized population of
the world. Half of the world's population lives in deep poverty and most of the
time their voices are absent at the highest levels of international policy making.

Literature Review

In today's world, refugees have become a threat to some countries' national security. In some parts of the world, refugees get amnesty and in the other parts of the world, they are not welcomed. But after reading further, I have learned that refugees lose their nationality once they leave their homeland and live in refugee camps, travel on boats or are put in detention centers. Furthermore, they do not have anyone to defend them, when sovereign states government or law enforcement officers confront them. Therefore, in my research project, I looked into two different case studies from the Americas and Africa. The first case is between Haitian refugees and the U.S. government. And the second case is between Sierra Leone refugees and the Republic of Guinea government. Although many scholars have written about international law and refugees, my independent research project tries to analyze if current international treaties or laws protect refugees outside their territory. The two case studies have many similarities and differences.

1) The Concept of International Law by Philip Allott:

In the beginning of the academic article, Philip Allot lays out three important factors of international law. First he says, "Law carries the structures and systems of society through time". Then he says, "Law inserts the common interest of society into the behavior of society-members". And finally he says, "Law establishes possible futures for society, in accordance with society's theories, values and purposes." The article recognizes the foundation of international law and how it relates to our global community. However, I did not find any words about how it is that this relates to refugees and the marginalized people of the world. For example, Allott says, "Law inserts the common interest of society into the behavior of society-members". How can this law be manifested in refugee camps? Refugees are not part of any society once they leave their homeland and move to go to another place. On the other hand, I agree with Allott about international society as a constitution free zone. Furthermore, he adds "Law was made to co-exist systemically with its ideal of justice." Even though international society is a constitution free zone, it should protect people from different walks of life. Justice should be at the core of local, national and international law.

2) Rethinking Refugee Law by Niraj Nathwani:

> In his book the author separates the idea between immigration law and refugee law. He states the following to support this tenant: "Immigration law is ruled by the principle of sovereignty, where every state is free to design and implement its own immigration policy, refugee law is characterized by various international obligations based on international law. While, under international law, a state is free to decide that it wishes no immigration, this level of discretion is not permitted under refugee law."

3) The 1951 Refugee Convention:

This 1951 convention, defining refugee status and characterizing the rights of refugees, determines in Article 31:

> "The Contracting States shall not impose penalties, on account of their illegal entry or presence, on refugees who, coming directly from a territory where their life or freedom was threatened in the sense of article 1, enter or are present in their territory without authorization, provided they present themselves without delay to the authorities and show good cause for their illegal entry or presence."

It is important to distinguish between the two issues. Refugees lack the diplomatic protection and they are internationally unprotected persons because they lack nationality just like stateless persons.

Methodology

I conducted my research project at the University for Peace in Ciudad Colón, Costa Rica. I conducted my research project at University for Peace because the institution has a strong focus on international law and human rights. Furthermore, University for Peace brings students and scholars from all over the world providing me with an opportunity to engage with students and scholars about my research project.

For my research project, I used case studies and biography methodology to conduct the project. The reason I wanted to use case studies and biography methodology to do the research is that it allows me to go to the library to do research, attend classes, and interview students and scholars about my subject. Finally, I analyzed two different refugee case studies from Africa and Americas.

To carry out my project, I was a participant and active researcher in the field. I spent a few hours everyday in the library and also in classes with the students. Being active in the classroom with the students enriched my experience at University for Peace and my project.

One of the most important parts of my research project was conducting interviews with the students and scholars. I interviewed two students and the Global College's field trip coordinator.

Interview Questions:

1. What's your name, Where are you from? (City/Town and Country)

2. What's your major?

3. What's your academic focus here at UPEACE?

4. How old are you? Male or Female?

5. Do you think the current international law protects refugees? If yes, can you give me an example?

6. From your perspective, what are the main reason refugees flee your country?

7. What do you think is the solution for refugee's issue?

8. What's the role of individual in helping refugees?

Sources of International Refugee Law

What is a refugee? Under the United Nations Convention Relating to the Status of Refugees 1951, in Article 1.A(2), a refugee is "owing to a well- founded fear of being persecuted for reasons of race, religion, nationality, membership of a particular social group, or political opinion, is outside the country of his nationality, and is unable to or, owing to such fear, is unwilling to avail himself of the protection of that country." The United Nations 1951 Convention Relating to the Status of Refugees restricted refugee status to those whose circumstances had come about "as a result of events occurring before 1 January 1951" and it gave states the option of interpreting the Convention as "events occurring in Europe or elsewhere." However, the 1967 Protocol Relating to the Status of Refugees had removed temporal and geographical restrictions. Furthermore, the concept of a refugee has been expanded after the 1967 Protocol and by regional conventions in Africa and the Americas.

The internationally accepted definition of refugee found in the 1951 Convention and the 1967 Protocol Relating to the Status of Refugees, has shown lacking meaning in dealing with refugees in Africa and the Americas. For instance, under the 1969 Organization of African Unity Convention Governing the Specific Aspects of Refugee Problems in Africa (OAU Convention), in Article 1(2), a ""refugee" shall also apply to every person who, owing to external aggression, occupation, foreign domination or events seriously disturbing public order in either part or the whole of his country of origin or nationality, is compelled to leave his place of habitual residence in order to seek refuge in another place outside his country of origin or nationality. Under the Cartagena Declaration on Refugees, a refugee is "persons who fled their country because their lives, safety or freedom have been threatened by generalized violence, foreign aggression, internal conflicts, massive violation of human rights or other circumstances which have seriously disturbed public order." These two conventions offer examples of the political injustices, occupations and internal conflicts that occurred and continue to occur in the two regions.

There are five relevant grounds for persecution, all of which in varying degrees, have been correspondingly developed in the field of non-discrimination.

Race is one of the important factors in the five relevant grounds for persecution. The authors of "The Refugee in International Law" write, "The International Criminal Tribunals note a shift towards the greater use of 'subjective criteria', including self-perception and the perception of others; the tribunals are.... Beginning to acknowledge that collective identities, and in particular ethnicity, are by their very nature social constructs, imagined identities entirely dependent on variable and contingent perceptions, and not social facts, which are verifiable in the same manner as natural phenomena or physical facts."

Religion is also an important factor in the five relevant grounds for persecution. The authors of "The Refugee in International Law" argue that, 'Religion', The Declaration on the Elimination of All forms of intolerance and of discrimination based on religion or belief, adopted in 1981 indicates the interests to be protected, the infringement of which may signal persecution.

Nationality is crucial in the 1951 Convention and in the 1967 Protocol Relating to the Status of Refugees. The authors of "The Refugee in International Law" argue that, 'Nationality', however, nationality in 1A(2) of the 1951 convention is usually interpreted more loosely to include origins and the membership of particular ethnic, religious, cultural and linguistic communities.

Gender is a vital part in the ground for persecution. The authors of "The Refugee in International Law" argue that, although the principle of non-discrimination on the ground of sex is now well established in international law, gender was not included in article 1A(2) as the basis for a well- founded fear of persecution. Furthermore, the authors argue that, "The 1993 UN Declaration on the Elimination of Violence against Women, moreover, acknowledges that all states have an obligation to work towards its eradication-- – Rape by a solider, policeman, or person in authority, for example, may be characterized as the unauthorized private act of an individual and therefore not persecution.

Post-World War II era, Latin American leaders gathered in Bogotá, Colombia to adopt the American Declaration of the Rights and Duties of Man. The American Declaration of the Rights and Duties of Man became effective in April 1948 and several months later, the Universal Declaration of Human Rights adopted in Palais de Chaillot Paris in December 1948. In fact, Latin American leaders were the largest regional blocs at the United Nations conference. The delegates from Latin America made sure the final draft of the American Declaration of the Rights and Duties of Man were incorporated into the Universal Declaration of Human Rights . On the one hand, with the regard to the status relating to refugees, the two conventions have similar approach to the protection of refugees. In fact, Article 27, under the American Declaration of the Rights and Duties of Man states that, "Every person has the right in case of pursuit not resulting from ordinary crimes, to seek and receive asylum in foreign territory, in accordance with the laws of each country and with international agreements." On the other hand, under the Universal Declaration of Human Rights, Article 14, states that, "Everyone has the right to seek and to enjoy in other countries asylum from persecution." The 1951 Convention Relating to the Status of Refugees and the 1967 Protocol Relating to the Status of Refugees has played a major role in the international and regional levels.

The principle of non-refoulement constitutes the cornerstone of international refugee's protection. It is protected in Article 33 (1) of the 1951 Convention, which is, "No Contracting State shall expel or return ("refouler") a refugee in any manner whatsoever to the frontiers of territories where his [or her] life or freedom would be threatened on account of his [or her] race, religion, nationality, membership of a particular social group or political opinion." States' non-refoulement obligations with respect to refugees are also established in the 1969 OAU Convention Governing Specific Aspects of Refugee problem in Africa and the 1969 American Convention on Human Rights.

Under the 1969 OAU Convention Governing Specific Aspects of Refugee problem in Africa, it is enshrined in Article 2 (1), which provides, "No person shall be subjected by a Member State to measures such as rejection at the frontier, return or expulsion, which would compel him to return to or remain in a territory where his life, physical integrity or liberty would be threatened for the reasons set out in Article I, paras. 1 and 2." Similarly, under the American Convention on Human Rights, it is established in Article 22 (8), which presents, "In no case may an alien be deported or returned to a country, regardless of whether or not it is his country of origin, if in that country his right to life or personal freedom is in danger of being violated because of his race, nationality, religion, social status, or political opinions."

Finally, with regard to non-refoulement, I will mention the United Nations Convention Against Torture. Under the United Nations Convention Against Torture, it is enshrined in Article 3 (1), "No State Party shall expel,return ("refouler") or extradite a person to another State where there are substantial grounds for believing that he would be in danger of being subjected to torture." In my next chapters in the essay, I will analyze and evaluate the international law violations among the different groups. Before, I conclude chapter two, I would like to give a difference between illegal or legal immigrants and refugees.

There is debate within the field of international migration question, if refugees are distinctively different from immigrants. In his academic journal, "Refugees, Immigrants, and the State", Jeremy Hein writes, "Immigrants constituted an economic form of migration, refugees a political form of migration."

Salve v. Haitian Center Council

In Haiti, during the dictatorships of François Duvalier and his son, Jean-Claude Duvalier, human rights violations were common in the country. During the terms of François Duvalier and Jean-Claude Duvalier, more than 100,000 Haitians were exiled and 30,000 killed. In 1991, Haiti chose its first democratically elected President, Jean-Bertrand Aristide, in 187 years of independence. In spite of his popular support, he was ousted by Haitian military in his first year. In the course of the military coup, many Haitians were tortured and killed. Therefore, many of them had been forced to flee the country. While many Haitians fled for personal safety and other fled for impoverished conditions; many Haitians fled to the United States for personal, political and economical safety. The United States government officials and Haitian government officials had diplomatic talk about mass migration to the U.S.

The United States government and Haitian government exchanged letters in 1981 regarding the mass Haitians migration to the United States. The letters allowed the U.S. Coast Guard to stop any Haitian vessels and detain any individuals suspected to attempting to enter the country illegally. Furthermore, President Regan issued an executive order to 'return' those Haitians who don't qualify under the definition of "refugee" under the 1951 UN Convention Relating to the Status of Refugees. The United States government argued that the 1951 Convention does not include those who flee for economic reasons. Finally, in 1992, President Bush issued an executive order declaring Article 33 of the 1951 Convention did not extend to individuals located beyond U.S. territory. In fact, according to the United Nations High Commission for Refugees, the United States is the first nation to ever implement such a policy.

The standard way of thinking about the Universal Declaration of Human Rights has been that every nation accepts the articles under the Universal Declaration of Human Rights. The United States as a member of the general assembly and a signatory to the Universal Declaration of Human Rights is bind to follow the articles. However, the United States government had violated Article 14(1) under the Universal Declaration of Human Rights. Article 14(1) which states that, "Every person has the right to seek and to enjoy in other countries asylum from persecution." One of the arguments that the United States presented was that the 1951 Convention did not include those who flee for economic conditions. Although I agree with the United States up to a point, I cannot accept their overall conclusion that the 1951 Convention does not include those who flee for economic conditions. The United States overlooks what I consider an important point about Haitians' situation. Haiti is the poorest nation in the Western Hemisphere and most of the refugees flee for economic and political conditions. I believe it is very hard to separate economic and political in the case of Haitians. For instance, many Haitians fled in the 1990s because of the oppressive military rule and lack of economic opportunity.

The United States government argued that the 1951 Convention does not apply to high seas outside of U.S territory. However, Article 33(1) of the 1951 Convention states, which is, "No Contracting State shall expel or return ("refouler") a refugee in any manner whatsoever to the frontiers of territories where his [or her] life or freedom would be threatened on account of his [or her] race, religion, nationality, membership of a particular social group or political opinion." By focusing on the 1951 Convention, the United States overlooks the deeper problem of Haitian refugees. These refugees fled their country because political instability, oppression, and other catastrophe.

The Convention Against Torture also includes a non-refoulement provision and uses the phrase "return" in Article 3(1). Article 3(1) states that, "No State

Party shall expel, 'return' ("refouler") or extradite a person to another State where there are substantial grounds for believing that he would be in danger of being subjected to torture." The United States government and the United States' Supreme Court violate three international treaties. The first is the Universal Declaration Human Rights, and the second one is the 1951 Convention/1967 Protocol. Finally, it violates the Convention Against Torture. The U.S. is a signatory and participated in the formation of all these treaties.

Ultimately, what is at stake here is the suffering of poor Haitian children, women, and men. They fled their country to improve their life, however, the U.S. government did not let them into the country. Ultimately, government officials, NGO officials and other politicians need to deal with refugees in micro level because sometimes women, children, and elderly do not have same power as young men and adult men. While I was doing research at the University for Peace, I asked a Bulgarian student from the Gender Department, if the current international law protects refugees? She replied, "It is not orientated with gender sensitivity. The women's issues are marginalized and put in the side in the mainstream discourse about refugees". Finally, it is important to be specific when United Nations High Commission for Refugees deal with refugees because officials need to stop to marginalize women, elder, children, disables.

African Institute for Human Rights and Development v. Guinea

Sierra Leone's eight-year civil war had devastated the country's natural resources and human resources. The civil war broke out in 1991 was a complex and brutal conflict. It had its roots in misrule government, neighbor country civil war, diamond wealth, and resentment poor rural against the richer ruling class. The war was fought between pro-government forces and a rebel forces. The guerilla war had a horrific method to terrorize people in the country. The war ended at the beginning of the 21st century.

In September 2000, Guinean President Lansana Conte declared over the national radio that Sierra Leone refugees were arrested, confined, and sent to refugee camps. Furthermore, in his speech he provoked soldiers and civilians to discriminate against Sierra Leone refugees. Furthermore, the complaint argues any attempt by Sierra Leone refugees to seek local remedies would be useless for three reasons. First, the author writes, "the need to exhaust domestic remedies is not necessarily required if the complainant is in a life-threatening situation that makes domestic remedies unavailable". Then, the author writes, "In September of 2000, Guinea hosted nearly 300 000 refugees from Sierra Leone. Given the mass scale of crimes committed against Sierra Leonean refugees -- 5 000 detentions, mob violence by Guinean security forces, widespread looting -- the domestic courts would be severely overburdened if even a slight majority of victims chose to pursue legal redress in Guinea. Consequently, the requirement to exhaust domestic remedies is impractical". Finally, the author writes, "exhausting local remedies would require Sierra Leonean victims to return to Guinea, the country in which they suffered persecution, a situation that is both impractical and unadvisable". Sierra Leone refugees had nowhere to run to and most of them fled to Guinea as a safe haven. However, a signatory, Guinea had a responsibility to follow international treaties and regional treaties among refugees.

On an international level, Guinea had violated the 1951 Convention Relating to the Status of Refugees and 1967 Protocol. Guinea had violated Article 3 in the 1951 Convention, which states, "The Contracting States shall apply the provisions of this Convention to refugees without discrimination as to race, religion or country of origin." In addition, Guinea also violated Article 33(1) which states, "No Contracting State shall expel or return ("refouler") a refugee in any manner whatsoever to the frontiers of territories where his life or freedom would be threatened on account of his race, religion, nationality, membership of a particular social group or political opinion."

Finally, Guinea had violated the Convention Against Torture. Article 3(1) in the Convention Against Torture, which states that, "No State Party shall expel, return ("refouler") or extradite a person to another State where there are substantial grounds for believing that he would be in danger of being subjected to torture." Even though Guinea is a signatory to all of those treaties and laws, Guinea did not hesitate to violate the treaties. During my two weeks research project, I interviewed few students about their perspectives on international law and its protection toward refugees. Adolphe Kilomba, a student from the Democratic Republic of Congo at the University for Peace in the International Law and Settlements of Disputes said, "A given state takes responsibility in its laws. A state needs to take serious measures in the international law". The republic of Guinea had also violated regional treaties as well.

Guinea had violated the 1969 Organization of African Unity Convention Governing The Specific Aspects of Refugee Problems in Africa.

In fact, it had violated two important articles. First, is Article 2(3) which states, "No person shall be subjected by a Member State to measures such as rejection at the frontier, return or expulsion, which would compel him to return to or remain in a territory where his life, physical integrity or liberty would be threatened for the reasons set out in Article I, paragraphs 1 and 2." The second is Article 4, which states, "Member States undertake to apply the provisions of this Convention to all refugees without discrimination as to race, religion, nationality, membership of a particular social group or political opinions." Although this case may seem insignificant, it is in fact crucial in terms of today's concern over Middle East and North African countries. For example, many Libyans fled to Europe and other African nations in search for safety. These two cases will have significant applications in the future international refugee law as well as in regional refugee law. To put it another way, how a nation deals with growing global issues.

Conclusion

My goal for this project was to learn how to protect refugees in the regional level and the international level. The two case studies I have looked at and analyzed gave me two different views about refugees' situation. On the one hand, I see there are many treaties and laws in the world. On the other hand, they are not respected or taken serious by some states in a time of urgent. Although I understand it is a very tough decision to make for host nations, when it comes to catastrophe, war, and natural disasters it becomes necessary to ensure the safety and the human rights of people.

I believe there is a long way to go in helping refugees and protect their human rights. In addition, the United Nations needs to enforce sovereign states to follow-up with their decision in different treaties. Even though states sign a treaty in the regional or international level, they do not abide by the laws. I firmly argue that there needs to a body at the United Nations that pressures countries to follow and act upon their words.

Bibliography

Allott, Philip, "The concept of international law" < http://www.ejil.org/
pdfs/10/1/577.pdf>

" The concept of international law" < http://www.ejil.org/pdfs/10/1/577.pdf>

Nathwani ,Niraj "Rethinking Refugee Law" Google Books < http://books.
google.com/books?id=jKD0nkOb1V oC&printsec=frontcover&
dq=refugees+law&hl=en&ei=809ZTdOwG4O88ga4-
MCrBw&sa=X&oi=book_result&ct=result&resnum=2&sqi=2&ved=0CDIQ
6AEwAQ#v=onepage&q=refugees%20law&f=false>

"Rethinking Refugee Law" Google Books < http://books.google.
com/books?id=jKD0nkOb1V oC&printsec=frontcover&
dq=refugees+law&hl=en&ei=809ZTdOwG4O88ga4-
MCrBw&sa=X&oi=book_result&ct=result&resnum=2&sqi=2&ved=0CDIQ
6AEwAQ#v=onepage&q=refugees%20law&f=false>

United Nations High Commission for Refugees, 1951 Convention/1967 Protocol,
< http://www.unhcr.org/protect/PROTECTION/3b66c2aa10.pdf>

United Nations High Commission for Refugees, 1951 Convention/1967 Protocol,
< http://www.unhcr.org/protect/PROTECTION/3b66c2aa10.pdf>

1969 Organization of African Unity Convention Governing The Specific Aspects
Refugee Problems in Africa, < http://www.africa- union.org/Official_
documents/Treaties_%20Conventions_%20Protocols/Ref ugee_Convention.
pdf>

United Nations High Commission for Refugees, Cartgena Declaration, < http://
www.unhcr.org/basics/BASICS/45dc19084.pdf>

"The Refugee in International Law", Guy S. GoodWin-Gill, and Jane Mcadam

The Universal Declaration of Human Rights and Latin America, Liliana, Obregon,
4/19/2009, < 26 http://www.law.umaryland.edu/academics/journals/mjil/
documents/vol_24_ 10.pdf>

Organization of American States, American Declaration of The Rights And Duties of Man, < http://www.oas.org/dil/1948%20American%20Declaration%20 of%20the%2 0Rights%20and%20Duties%20of%20Man.pdf>

Universal Declaration of Human Rights, < http://www.un.org/en/documents/ udhr/index.shtml>

United Nations High Commission for Refugees, 1951 Convention/1967 Protocol, < http://www.unhcr.org/protect/PROTECTION/3b66c2aa10.pdf>

1969 Organization of African Unity Convention Governing The Specific Aspects Refugee Problems in Africa, < http://www.africa- union.org/Official_ documents/Treaties_%20Conventions_%20Protocols/Ref ugee_Convention. pdf>

American Convention on Human Rights, < http://www.wunrn.com/reference/pdf/ American_convention_Human_Rights .PDF>

United Nation Convention Against Torture, < http://www.hrweb.org/legal/cat.html>

Refugees, Immigrants and the State, Academic Jouranl (JSTOR), Jeremy Hein

Fordham International Law Journal, Salve v Haitian Centers Council: The Return of Haitian Refugees, Andrew G. Pizor, 1993, < http://ir.lawnet.fordham.edu/ cgi/viewcontent.cgi?article=1393&context=ilj& sei-redir=1#search=%22sale+ v+haitian+centers+council+pdf%22>

Fordham International Law Journal, Salve v Haitian Centers Council: The Return of Haitian Refugees, Andrew G. Pizor, 1993, < http://ir.lawnet.fordham.edu/ cgi/viewcontent.cgi?article=1393&context=ilj& sei-redir=1#search=%22sale+ v+haitian+centers+council+pdf%22>

Fordham International Law Journal, Salve v Haitian Centers Council: The Return of Haitian Refugees, Andrew G. Pizor, 1993, < http://ir.lawnet.fordham.edu/ cgi/viewcontent.cgi?article=1393&context=ilj& sei-redir=1#search=%22sale+ v+haitian+centers+council+pdf%22>

Fordham International Law Journal, Salve v Haitian Centers Council: The Return of Haitian Refugees, Andrew G. Pizor, 1993, < http://ir.lawnet.

fordham.edu/cgi/viewcontent.cgi?article=1393&context=ilj& sei-redir=1#se arch=%22sale+v+haitian+centers+council+pdf%22>

Universal Declaration of Human Rights, < http://www.un.org/en/documents/ udhr/index.shtml>

United Nations High Commission for Refugees, 1951 Convention/1967 Protocol, < http://www.unhcr.org/protect/PROTECTION/3b66c2aa10.pdf>

United Nation Convention Against Torture, < http://www.hrweb.org/legal/cat.html>

" A country torn by conflict" Caroline Hawley, Tuesday 12, 1999 < http://news. bbc.co.uk/2/hi/special_report/1999/01/99/sierra_leone/251377.st m>

Compendium of Key Human Rights Documents of African Union, Christof Heyns and Magnus Killander < http://www.pulp.up.ac.za/cat_2010_11.html>

United Nations High Commission for Refugees, 1951 Convention/1967 Protocol, < http://www.unhcr.org/protect/PROTECTION/3b66c2aa10.pdf>

United Nations High Commission for Refugees, 1951 Convention/1967 Protocol, < http://www.unhcr.org/protect/PROTECTION/3b66c2aa10.pdf> United Nation Convention Against Torture, http://www.hrweb.org/legal/cat.html>

1969 Organization of African Unity Convention Governing The Specific Aspects Refugee Problems in Africa, < http://www.africa- union.org/Official_documents/ Treaties_%20Conventions_%20Protocols/Ref ugee_Convention.pdf>

1969 Organization of African Unity Convention Governing The Specific Aspects Refugee Problems in Africa, < http://www.africa- union.org/Official_ documents/Treaties_%20Conventions_%20Protocols/Ref ugee_Convention.pdf>

The Rise of Right Wing Nationalism in Hungary

Discussing Hungary's dueling political parties and assesses the rise of the right-wing FIDESZ party and the Jobbik movement.

Martin Dimitrov
University of Glasgow, written while studying at Hong Kong University

Abstract

Hungary, once seen as a poster child for democracy, is now enduring the effects of curbed political speech and the rise of a powerful right-wing nationalism. In this essay, the author investigates Hungary's dueling political parties and comes to assess the rise of the right-wing FIDESZ party and the Jobbik movement. The author finds the ascension of these groups worrisome, arguing they've limited political freedoms and are compounding Hungary's sociopolitical problems.

A strange occurrence is taking place in Europe during the last two years. While the Western media outlets transmit the voices and images of the liberating Arab peoples who overthrow one authoritarian regime after another, the very opposite trend is being observed in the heart of Europe, where the Hungarian Parliament is passing laws restricting the freedom of speech and information, curbing the political independence of the state judiciary and merging the state regulators of the financial markets with the central bank, thus centralizing the control over the monetary supply.[1] The country, which used to be regarded as a benchmark of post-socialist transition and a vanguard stable democracy in the region is now being condemned by the European Parliament and the IMF. "… With a nationalist strongman on the helm, the economy in shambles, and a ferocious far right both in its parliament and in black uniforms patrolling its suburbs[2]," Hungary may even become the first European country where radio Free Europe, the station airing uncensored news through the Iron Curtain during the Soviet times, may reinitiate its transmissions.[3] These controversial trends have been attributed to the emergence of the Centre-right Conservative FIDESZ party led by the charismatic Victor Orban which holds 68% of the seats in Parliament. Another worrying trend is the rising support of the Jobbik movement, a far-right anti-establishment, anti-Roma party preaching extreme nationalism and closely linked to the banned paramilitary Hungarian Guard.

In order to explore this anti-liberal, nationalistic upbeat in Hungarian politics, this essay will approach the question from two sides. First of all, emphasis will be put on the domestic political trends which brought to the rising support of the Right, beginning with the total loss of credibility due to allegations of corruption and public deceptions of the Left-wing MSZP party governing the country between 2002 and 2010. Afterwards a brief account of the development of FIDESZ will be given, with an emphasis on the intra-party centralization and mobilization during crucial periods of the last 20 years. Finally, attention will be turned to the general trends of the post-Communist Hungarian politics which induced the unprecedented rise of a single party, including the personalization of the political choice, the distrust of parties and the cracks in the seemingly stable electoral system of the country. Secondly, attention will be turned to the external preconditions of the rise of right-wing national conservatives, emphasizing on the European-wide trend of increasing far-right support due to the economic downturn which had brought popular feeling of disillusionment with the established free-market, liberal values framework of politics in the Old Continent. It will be argued that the simultaneous combination of these political trends, institutional preconditions and economic realities had brought to the controversial rise of the Right in Hungary.

"There is not much choice... No European country has done something as boneheaded as we have...We have obviously lied throughout the past one and a half - two years. It was perfectly clear that what we were saying was not true. We are beyond the country's possibilities to such an extent..." –Ferenc Gyurcsany's "Lying Speech" of 2006

There is little question that one of the main reasons for that one of the core reasons for the rise of the Right in Hungary was the ultimate failure of the Left during their 8 years in power from 2002 to 2010. Mismanagement of public funds and inconsistent macroeconomic decisions brought to the collapse of the heavy industry of the state, leaving the country with the record 11.2% of the working population being unemployed, the highest figure since 1992 and enormous public deficit requiring emergency funding of $25 billion from the IMF in 2008.[4] What is more, the speech served as a public admittance of the deceptions employed by the Socialist party in order to secure victory and re-election in 2006.[5] Additionally, this was perceived as hypocrisy on behalf of the governing party and led to mass anti-governmental protests in the autumn of 2006, which served well the already gaining momentum FIDESZ party.

The rise of the so-called Civic Circles, anti-left civil society groupings before the 2006 elections did not manage to help Orban win the struggle with MSZP undisputedly, but showed the strength of the Conservative party to ride the tide of popular disillusionment and to amass tens of thousands of activists within weeks[6] and was employed once again amidst the protests after the scandalous speech. However, this is not the first time Orban and his party manages to adjust to the situation and extract the maximum out of the trends of mass distrust in what is seen as stagnating, corrupt current order. Starting as a revolutionary dissident movement in the late 1980s, FIDESZ started as an anti-establishment faction of the Hungarian Democratic Forum, which strongly opposed the communist system and values of multiculturalism and emphasized the importance of national values.[7] The first change of faces came in the first years of transition, when the radical façade was dropped down, allowing for the conformity with the established multiparty order and paving the "third way" of liberal – conservative politics, a combination of issues of ecology and women's rights with nationalism, Christian values and protectionist economics.[8] Slowly but steadily, with the failures in each elections cycle of the early 1990s, the ideological axis was swinging away from the initial liberal core to a rhetoric of nativist, national interest and conservatism, filling the gap in the Centre-Right of Hungarian politics.[9] This change of hearts won FIDESZ the 1998 elections and the government of Orban showed its inclination towards centralization of power by passing an administrative reform extending the capabilities of the cabinet at the expense of the power of the ministries.[10] Although its cabinet fell out of grace due to allegations of corruption, FIDESZ gained a new, professionalized political face and a momentum of popular support, which got employed several times during their years in opposition, giving the popular disdain towards the Socialist government "political leadership and to seek to channel them into a coherent political objective."[11] By siding with the people in times when the majority is experiencing the negative economic effects of a global crisis, by taking strong and distinctive stances on currently relevant issues and opposing the perceived perpetrators of the crisis – the current liberal international economic order, globalization and the party that embraced these values – the MSZP, FIDESZ won the support of the majority by a landslide. But it was not only Orban's party that rode on the discontent of the people. Employing a slightly different, more radical rhetoric and adding the upholding of law, order, national centrism and security against the perceived threat of Roma crime in the rural areas of the state[12] to FIDESZ recipe outlined above, Jobbik won 12% of the vote in 2010. Invoking the thought of national disasters

The combination of failure of a corrupt Left and mobilization of a centralized, paternalistic Right, although treated by this essay as symptoms of the assurgency of the latter on the expense of the failure of the former, can also be observed as consequences of the manner in which politics in Hungary have institutionalized in the post-Communist era. First of all, although officially parliamentarian, the Hungarian system suffers from what Juan Linz had called "The perils of Presidentialism" in 1990[13], or what is the problem of too personalized style of politics in which parties and ideology come second after the image and charisma of their leaders. Polls say that for Hungarians the most distrusted entities in the political spectrum are the political parties, which lag behind the constitutional court, the president and the parliament, with only between 25% and 36% of the people trusting them between 2006 and 2010.[14] The most perilous effect of such politics is the self-identification of the people with a single political figure, which gives the individual legitimacy when elected, otherwise reserved to a broad coalition of people, sharing the same ideology, but preserving their individual views.[15] Although the system seems apparently stable, with a standard 5% threshold for a party to get elected into parliament and electoral rules privileging bigger parties expected to form stable governments, the most recent election results showed that even well-established systems are vulnerable to populism and may pave the way for anti-democratic sentiments.[16]

However, the internal political and socio-economic reasons behind the assurgency of the Right in Hungary examined up until now, undeniably important and crucial to the understanding of this issue, are to be put into an international context in order to be comprehended fully. Currently, the support of conservative and far-right parties is on the rise throughout Europe – the Freedom Party in Austria, the Swedish Democrats, the True Fins as well as the Danish People's Party, who share common political believes with Jobbik, are examples that ultranationalist groups may emerge even in the some of the oldest established and highly regarded European democracies.[17] The shared values of these parties including distrust of globalization and Europeanization, intolerance towards immigrant, seen as job-stealers (in the Eastern European cases – the Roma, seen as anti-social, unable to integrate and unjustly reliant on welfare support) and opposition to liberal social and market views increase their appeal during times of economic calamities.[18] Figures speak for themselves in the case of Hungary – according to a special report by the European Bank of Reconstruction and Development, Hungarian's faith in free markets has dropped with 10% and that in democracy – with 6% in the last 4 years, while 60% of the population blames the West for its perilous circumstances.[19] The Nobel Prize winner Paul Krugman warns of the devastating effects an economic crisis can have on current political realm of Europe, where the instability of the Euro, requiring austerity measures (in addition to the crippled consumption means) to ensure its survival, is opposed by euro-skepticism and retreat to nationalism[20] – precisely the medicine offered by FIDESZ, and to a more radical extent – Jobbik.

"Populist practices emerge out of the failure of existing social and political institutions to confine and regulate political subjects into a relatively stable social order. It is the language of politics when there can be no politics as usual... It is a political appeal that seeks to change the terms of political discourse, articulate new social relations, redefine political frontiers and constitute new identities." [21]

To a great extent, what Panizza summarizes so eloquently is what Hungarian Politics passes through at that very moment. The grim economic downturn, perceivably imported from the outside, had sprawled mass disillusionment with globalization, free markets ideology and democracy, which have been linked to the problems of the Hungarian society and had resulted into a retreat to the national values, traditions and interests. The agile and flexible Right had successfully adjusted to the popular sentiments and fears, flattering the majority (in the case of FIDESZ) and turning against the "outsiders" – Roma and the international system (in the case of Jobbik).[22] Combined with the deep distrust in the MSZP due to 8 years of corruption and economic mismanagement, the power of the Right had erupted in the last elections. The catalyst had been the institutional framework of politics in the form of electoral laws presupposing personalized, winner-takes-it-all politics. The combination of these institutional, political and economic preconditions had brought the total domination of the Right in Hungary at this moment.

Bibliography

Day, Matthew (2010) "Rise of Hungary's far-Right Jobbik party stirs disturbing echoes of the 1940s"- The Telegraph, Published 03.04.2010, Accessed 19.03.2012, URL: http://www.telegraph.co.uk/news/worldnews/europe/hungary/7549950/Rise-of-Hungarys-far-Right-Jobbik-party-stirs-disturbing-echoes-of-the-1940s.html

European Bank for Reconstruction and Development Report Transition Report 2011- "Crisis in Transition: The People's Perspective" – Published 15.11.2011, Accessed 19.03.2012, URL: http://www.ebrd.com/pages/research/publications/flagships/transition.shtml

Gyurcsány, Ferenc (2006) – Speech in Balatonőszöd, Accessed 21.03.2012, URL: http://en.wikipedia.org/wiki/Ferenc_Gyurcs%C3%A1ny's_speech_in_ Balaton%C5%91sz%C3%B6d_in_May_2006#cite_note-1

Hockenos , Paul (2011) "On the March - Hungary's Ascendant Right Wing" – Boston Review, Published July/August 2011, Accessed 21.03.2012, URL: http://www.bostonreview.net/BR36.4/paul_hockenos_hungary_europe_ right_wing_extremism.php

"Jobbik – Radical Change" (2010) Manifesto, Downloaded from http://jobbik.com/

Krugman, Paul (2011) "Depression and Democracy" – New York Times, Published 11.12.2011, Accessed 21.03.2012, URL: http://www.nytimes. com/2011/12/12/opinion/krugman-depression-and-democracy.html?_r=2

Linz, Juan (1990) "The Perils of Presidentialism", Journal of Democracy, Winter 1990 pp. 51-69

Mudde, Cas (2007) "Populist Radical Right Parties in Europe", Cambridge University Press, UK

Palmer ,Mark, Haraszti , Miklos and Gati , Charles (2012) "Support democracy in Hungary with new Radio Free Europe broadcasts", The Washington Post, Published 27.02.2012, Accessed 19.03.2012, URL: http://www. washingtonpost.com/opinions/support-democracy-in-hungary-with-new- radio-free-europe-broadcasts/2012/02/17/gIQAI7KdcR_story.html

Panizza, Francisco (2005) "Populism and the mirror of democracy ", London: Verso

Porter, Anna (2010) "The ghosts of Europe: Central Europe's past and uncertain future", New York, St. Martin's Press

Schöpflin , György (2007) "Democracy, populism, and the political crisis in Hungary" – Eurozine, Published 07.05.2007, Accessed 20.03.2012, URL: http://www.eurozine.com/articles/2007-05-07-schopflin-en.html

Szabó, Máté(2011) "From a Suppressed Anti-Communist Dissident Movement to a Governing Party: The Transformations of FIDESZ in Hungary", Corvinus Journal of Sociology and Social Policy Vol.2 (2011) 2, 47–66

Todosijevic , Bojan (2005) "Issues and Party Preferences in Hungary : A Comparison of Directional and Proximity Models" - Party Politics 2005 11: 109-126

Webb , Paul and White, Stephen (2007) "Party Politics in New Democracies" Oxford University Press, UK

Endnotes

1. Krugman, Paul (2011) "Depression and Democracy" – New York Times, Published 11.12.2011.

2. Hockenos , Paul (2011) "On the March - Hungary's Ascendant Right Wing" – Boston Review, Published July/August 2011.

3. Palmer ,Mark, Haraszti , Miklos and Gati , Charles (2012) "Support democracy in Hungary with new Radio Free Europe broadcasts", The Washington Post, Published 27.02.2012.

4. Day, Matthew (2010) "Rise of Hungary's far-Right Jobbik party stirs disturbing echoes of the 1940s"- The Telegraph, Published 03.04.2010, Accessed 19.03.2012.

5. Gyurcsány, Ferenc (2006) – Speech in Balatonőszöd, Accessed 21.03.2012.

6. 6 Webb , Paul and White, Stephen (2007) "Party Politics in New Democracies"

7. Todosijevic , Bojan (2005) "Issues and Party Preferences in Hungary : A Comparison of Directional and Proximity Models" - Party Politics 2005

8. Szabó, Máté(2011) "From a Suppressed Anti-Communist Dissident Movement to a Governing Party: The Transformations of FIDESZ in Hungary", Corvinus Journal of Sociology and Social Policy Vol.2 (2011)

9. Mudde, Cas (2007) "Populist Radical Right Parties in Europe"

10. Webb., Ibid.

11. Schöpflin , György (2007) "Democracy, populism, and the political crisis in Hungary" – Eurozine, Published 07.05.2007.

12. "Jobbik – Radical Change" (2010) Manifesto.

13. Linz, Juan (1990) "The Perils of Presidentialism", Journal of Democracy, Winter 1990.

14. Webb., Ibid.

15. Linz., Ibid.

16. Szabó., Ibid.

17. Porter, Anna (2010) "The ghosts of Europe: Central Europe's past and uncertain future"

18. Day., Ibid.

19. European Bank for Reconstruction and Development Report Transition Report 2011- "Crisis in Transition: The People's Perspective" – Published 15.11.2011.

20. Krugman., Ibid.

21. Panizza, Francisco (2005) "Populism and the mirror of democracy "

22. Muddle., Ibid.

globalcitizenjournal.org

Pour les étudiants du monde francophone qui avaient ecrit les mémoires exémplaires, envoyez le vôtre à globalcitizendakar@gmail.com pour qu'il puisse être consideré dans le prochain numéro de The Global Citizen: Dakar, le Bureau Français de The Global Citizen.

THE GLOBAL CITIZEN

A WORLDWIDE FORUM FOR INTERNATIONAL AFFAIRS

| Volume I | January 2013 | Issue 1 |